# Pandemic

## Break The Outbreak

By Don Adamson

Published by 4 Points Publishing©

Don Adamson

PO Box 651, Vandalia, OH  45377

www.4points.pub

www.acts29missions.org

eBook edition created 2020

Edited by Susan Cardinal

Cover by Laura Adamson     www.lauraadamson.com

ISBN 978-0-9964824-5-5

Dedication

I would like to dedicate this book to all the first responders, doctors, nurses, and the employees of essential businesses who have been under pressure like never before. Your courage and sacrifice aren't in secret. Only time will tell of the many heroes you all are.

.

bless·ed

/blest, ˈblesid/

- endowed with divine favor and protection.

- bringing pleasure or relief as a welcome contrast
  to what one has previously experienced.

Table of Contents

Salvation Message
About Don Adamson
About Acts 29 Missions

Page 6

# A Word Of Warning.

Some of this writing can be pretty intimidating as my audience is most probably American or Western culture. However, what can be more threatening than a pandemic that has upset everything we've known to be true? If COVID-19 hasn't directly affected you, one look at the news media, and you'll learn of our precarious position. In a short amount of time, we went from the powers that be, to helpless and exposed. To put it simply, we've gone from buying $40 scented candles to struggling to pay rent. God's Word tells us these times are coming.

Like the original disciples who had delusions of grandeur, we also fell into the trap of self-interest. We became too busy building our kingdoms to pay attention to the noise coming from abroad. And why not? Many months ago, we were singing, "Let the good times roll." But just like cancer that is growing silently under a layer of skin, we got caught unawares.

Of course, all is not lost because this event didn't catch God asleep at the helm. No, with His prediction, also came the solution. I want to approach this book as a Christian and offer a biblical answer. One that would steer us toward victory over such an overwhelming event called a pandemic. Like a microscope used to see a Coronavirus, I'm going to magnify three little verses in the book of Psalms. You will be surprised, like I was, how these small verses can pack a mighty punch to overcome a global plague, even to the destruction of a virus.

With the risk of sounding non-original, a couple of these stories are condensed versions of previous and future publications. My life seems to be peppered with supernatural events that cannot be explained any other way than by God. I picked the stories to prove a point in this day and hour of a global pandemic that is destroying the planet.

I also want to fuss about how we go through this as Americans. Fuss? Did I say fuss? Yes, I'm very familiar with Americans. I am one of them. But I also live in one of the most challenging countries on the earth today.

Since its founding in 1804, Haiti has been on one roller-coaster ride after another. Not only have devastating mistakes by men brought disaster to generations of Haitians, but even nature seems always to be angry. Earthquakes, hurricanes, endemics, violence, corruption, the list goes on and on. You wouldn't know unless you have experienced the country, but Haitians are some of the most exceptional people on the planet. Some great Christian believers there have faith to overcome obstacles that the Western World doesn't even consider. When I get a headache, I take an aspirin. But for Haitians, especially where I live in the remote mountain areas, they must believe God for everything. There are no hospitals, urgent care centers, or emergency rooms like we have here. If they had access to one, the care they would receive might kill them anyway. These are the people that I live with and observe how they approach a living God. Most of the people are illiterate. When we teach what the Bible says about faith and then match it with how they believe God, we see miracles.

I strongly encourage you that if you can get through chapter one without burning this book and taking me off your "friends" list on Facebook, you will unquestionably be inspired by the power coming from the following chapters. This revelation came as no surprise when it did. As you will read, it was a life and death declaration long before this virus came to our shores.

To observe a medical report given by qualified doctors to be disassembled by faith is no small thing. God loves us so much that He would reveal the answer to everything that would counterattack that love—even if it is a worldwide pandemic.

I'm trusting you will receive the same revelation I have. It is the power to break the outbreak. My earnest prayer is that our loving Savior is seen as our ever-present help in time of need. I believe that His protection, strengthening, and healing will be made manifest through the pages of this book.

- Don

# CHAPTER ONE

## Enter Into The Blessing

As the baby in the family, my dad would ask me to say the blessing at Thanksgiving dinner. I guess he thought that since I was the youngest, that whatever I blurted out in that prayer would be acceptable, even if it sounded awkward. But I had a secret weapon. The Cincinnati Enquirer would print a prayer the day before Thanksgiving. Of course, my mom would know what I was up to and always made sure a trip to the store was made before that edition would run out. To say the blessing before we ate our Thanksgiving dinner meant all I had to do was bow my head, fold my hands, keep one eye open, and read the pre-printed prayer that I had on my lap. No matter what year I prayed it, the prayer always started and ended something like this; "Lord, we ask thy blessing…and now we thank thee for thy blessing."

 Fast forward a few decades, and my prayers are still basically the same. So many events, decisions, and yes, sin, should have destroyed me. Or at least embarrassed me in front of the people whom I love. When I would get out of a scrape, it was like I wiped the sweat off my forehead and exclaim, "Whew, now that was close…thank you Lord for blessing me!" It's not that something suddenly would materialize that I would blurt out such a thing. It was usually the other way around when anguish was at my doorstep. Somehow, someway, there was this force around me where it was easy for me to thank God Almighty for the blessing from something that could end my life. We all look for that "power" that goes before us as the angels are sent on assignment when we wake up in the morning. Many in the church ask, "where is that power in such a desperate time?" Well, I found it! I promise by the end of these few pages, you will too. It's real, alive, and ready to take on any assignment heaven sends it to.

Events in my life would happen that would be wonderful, supernatural, unexpected...and obviously, a blessing. I know the Bible says much about how much God loves us and wants the best for His children. The book of Luke says,

"...it is the Father's good pleasure to give us the kingdom."

Luke 12:32

And what a kingdom it is! One day I found myself with significant needs, and the next, I had more than enough. How incredibly upside down and inside out the kingdom can be. It sometimes looks opposite to what we have been taught.

If you have ever followed one of my books, blogs, social media posts, or joined me in the mountains of the mission field, you would quickly understand that word "opposite." The way Jesus walked into my bedroom one night and delivered me from the damage of the pornography business, He showed me what would be the foundation of my life. Not mine only, but the vision, ministry, and destiny He had for me to touch others. It is found in Genesis 50:20.

"But as for you, you meant evil against me; but God meant it for good, in order to bring it about as it is this day, to save many people alive." Gen50:20

In my book "The Jesus Of My Agony," I abbreviate it even more simply; "What's meant for harm, God turns for good." In my 2nd book titled "I Never Lose," I say it this way: "What's meant for harm, God turns for good." My 3rd publication says it like this; "What's meant for harm, God turns for good." In my next book, I spell it out like this "What's meant for harm, God turns for good."

So, you get the point. I'm sure you are thankful I didn't explain that in every post or conversation that I have made in social media circles. If I did, it would say the same. Are you ready for it? "What's meant for harm, God turns for good."

You can't change my mind. It has happened time and time again. Whether trouble came from my fellow humankind who decided to hurt me or a full-on attack from a demonic principality, that scripture is like a neon signpost pointing me towards victory. It is like a silver bullet in my gun that never misses its target. The Adamson Version of scripture would put it this way; "You shouldn't oughta gone and done that." I have been trained my entire Christian life that God can turn anything of harm for my good.

# A New Disaster

Disasters to someone like me seem to not have the same sting as most. Why would they? If you lived through as many of them as I have, you would have learned that Genesis 50:20 principle works. Working in Haiti can sometimes be trial by fire. No, I'm not Superman, who is impervious to pain and suffering caused by a disaster. It is that I have learned that if I would give God 'a minute' and apply my faith, He can turn it for my good.

Just one example would be our school in Haiti. In 2008/09, the world was recovering from a recession brought on by the stock market collapse. Soon after that, a 7.0 earthquake destroyed Port-Au-Prince. A Cholera epidemic quickly followed. During that time, I lost my best friend and translator to a motorcycle accident that left him mentally injured. One would think, amid disasters happening all around us, the natural thing would be to coast awhile and allow things to improve slowly. Yet, right in the middle of all of that, the Holy Spirit reveals to us that we are to build a school where there has never been a school. To the world, it doesn't make sense. But to God, He was just waiting for us to say "yes" to His timing.

Natural disasters have been a part of my life since I began our work in Haiti. But then 2019 came along, and a word that I have only heard in movies became alive to the entire world: pandemic. More specifically, the Coronavirus Pandemic. At first, it seemed to be on the other side of the world and life as

I knew it continued all the same. Christmas came and went. We greeted the New Year with excitement as we laid out several events for the year in Haiti. Suddenly, more and more reports started coming in from several areas in the United States. In all my experiences of spiritual warfare and seeing God's supernatural power bring me deliverance, this came at me sideways. I couldn't apply my knowledge of disaster relief as there was nothing in my vision that I could target my efforts. I couldn't lock-on my faith as it was an elusive enemy.

All the alarms were ringing in my head as it had every connotation and description of darkness and death. I have been through both more times than I care to mention in this book. Indeed, it would have been easier for me to envision a voodoo witchdoctor hell-bent on destroying my life, or the dark storm clouds of a hurricane rolling in, or even the earth shaking under my feet. At least that would have given me a focal point of my faith and prayers that could have helped me visualize the enemy.

But a virus? Not just that, but a virus that spreads from one person to another by merely breathing air. A dangerous microbe that had gone around the entire planet as fast as an airplane can take it. One look at the video on the news showed the seriousness of this microscopic enemy. All around the world, healthy, happy people had succumbed to this threat that we would typically think would only impact the elderly or immune-deficient. Surely that would be easier to accept. But that was not the case. It targeted: rich and poor, city and countryside, rainforest and desert, African, American, Asian, etc…it didn't seem to care. Every international, national, and local government gave daily reports to an enemy none could see. But the tally of destruction left behind was easy to count as the gravedigger's business picked up more and more. Who would have thought the term "flatten the curve" would now be an everyday saying?

## Pay It Forward

During this time, the Holy Spirit made it so very clear to me how I was to direct my faith so I wouldn't be walking around in some worldly fog, just waiting for the next statistics to come out. Even more so, it wasn't directed toward my principal scripture: "what was meant for harm, God turns for good," as I felt safe and healthy. In my prayer time, I could sense that He was leading me in a more proactive direction. Because of the way problems came at me in Haiti, I fell into this trap that something of "harm" had to personally show up so I could apply my faith to it being turned for my "good." It wasn't going to work that way because if this particular harm of the Coronavirus came to my family or me, it could take our lives quickly. It could even be invisibly ravaging our bodies, and we wouldn't have a clue. I had to be preemptive in my faith battle towards this new evil. Once I understood that revelation, my mind went back to a prayer meeting last fall when I prayed out

Psalm 41. I can't even tell you how or why I was in that area of the Bible. As I spoke that out, I felt a quickening in my spirit, and it started becoming more and more a part of my thought process. Suddenly I prayed it daily, and each time a building of revelation began to happen. I'm sure my prayer team was getting tired of me going after that scripture day after day, but I knew it was God directing me. He showed me these verses before the virus became a news story.

In what seemed like a few weeks, the pandemic began raging through the nations. The whole world sat on the edge of their seats when a news story came out about a vaccine. "A vaccine! A vaccine has been found! Were saved by a vaccine!" But the reality is that even if it was effective, it was many months down the road. The Holy Spirit was saying to me to operate NOW in this word, not later, as if I, too, was waiting for some medical breakthrough. He clearly has shown that this is the answer to a pandemic, such as we see now. The entire "What's meant for harm, God turns for good" is working as a Pay-It-Forward that is framed in 3 verses of Psalm 41. Another way of saying this is Psalm 41 preempts the harm that Genesis 50:20 needs to turn it to my good.

But the answer to a pandemic in Psalm 41:1-3 isn't automatic. No more than the harm-to-good principle in Genesis 50:20. You must apply your faith! If something meant for harm comes against us, God is not going to turn it for our good if we just eat, drink and be merry, all the while waiting for destruction to come. We must see that principle and then believe that it is actively providing a process that will lead to our success.

Could it be that the Word of God speaks explicitly about destroying the outbreak of a pandemic or plague? It sure does. Like sewing a coat of many colors, let me grab several verses of another Psalm, many of us know well. Psalm 91 seems to be our go-to Psalm when all hell breaks loose in our lives. I'll use the New Living Translation to make miscellaneous verses come together and read with more clarity. After reading this, it is easy to see that God *does* have something to say about pandemics. See for yourself:

"Do not dread the disease that stalks in darkness, nor the disaster that strikes at midday. Though ten thousand are dying around you, these evils will not touch you. No plague will come near your home". The Lord says, "I will rescue those who love me. I will protect those who trust in my name. I will reward them with a long life and give them my salvation."

Psalm 91 NLT (edits mine)

## What's Big Deal Of Psalm 41?

When this outbreak first arrived, if you thought like me, you would say let's stick to those power verses in Psalm 91. Or possibly some New Testament authority-packed scripture about the resurrection power of Jesus. That would surely pack more punch than a song by David in Psalms. Many of us picture the painting of a peaceful David playing the harp as he watched over his resting sheep. If that is our visual, we automatically fall into a feeble understanding of Psalm 41. Let me take verses 7 and 8 to disprove that notion. It lays out the reality that Psalm 41 isn't some tranquil poetic sheepherders' ballad, but a reality check of pain and betrayal. David minces no words as he speaks about those who wish him dead.

> All who hate me whisper together against me;
> they devise harm against me.
> "An evil disease clings to him.
> And now that he lies down, he will not rise up again."
> Psalm 41:7-8

Yes, some incredible scriptures scream to be declared in times like this. However, I cannot deny that these particular three verses in Psalm 41 showed up when they did, and brought miraculous results, long before this virus showed up.

You may know of the political unrest we had in Haiti at the closing months of 2019. It looked much like what we have seen in our American cities over the recent racial issues that have come up. Like in the USA, we had streets blocked with protesters wanting a change in the Haitian government.

Let me detail just ten days in the middle of all that unrest to show the capability of Psalm 41:1-3. During these times of riots, we came upon several roadblocks, but for some unknown reason, no criminals were manning the barricade. I saw a man who reached down to throw a big rock into my window. Suddenly, he froze and couldn't even get his arm to move forward. You could see the confusion that overtook his mind, as with a blank face, he just watched me drive by. On our way to the school, the entire bridge was obstructed with old cars on fire, yet, one truck got through that day. Can you guess whose? We underestimated a building project cost, and somehow, we still got the job done better than we expected. We buried our truck in a river, but it came right back out, and we found another way to cross over. We had an accident where a motorcycle drove too fast, bounced off my truck, skidded across a gravel road, and ran into a pile of cement blocks. After the dust cleared, they didn't even have a scratch. I have been in Haiti long enough to know that was a 4-hospital trip for the men on that bike. Even the American teams that were with me said they felt the favor of God as we went about the ministry in the mountain villages. Was it all luck? Was it just coincidence? Was I only in the right place at the right time? No, my friends. Psalm 41:1-3 was prayed, activated, and working in and around us daily.

## Proof Of The Power

Trucks in mud, driving through roadblocks, protection in ministry, those are great stories, but a complete undoing of a global pandemic might make you question this idea of the potency in Psalm 41. I'm not only going to agree with that reasoning as it seems much more significant. Yet, I'm also going to prove that without this Psalm, the entire resurrection of Jesus Christ would look different than what we know today. Let me bring that one power-scripture into clarity to prove my point about how critical this revelation is for this time we are living.

Picture in your mind the birth, life, death, and resurrection of Jesus as recorded in the Gospels. At the appointed time, Jesus came into the world and taught clearly who He was and what He came to accomplish, all with signs and wonders to back it up. He also knew when all of that was done, His time of departure was at hand. Everything was set for the ultimate sacrifice Jesus was going to pay on that hill called Calvary. Now there needed to be that one event that tipped the scales for Jesus to go to the cross. This one action was what Satan and all of hell gambled on for what they believed would be their ultimate victory. The pawn of this single event placed the responsibility on one man: Judas Iscariot. It all hinged on him. Now in the garden of Gethsemane, God laid upon Jesus the sins of the world. All the suffering that He was to pay to ransom our souls was before Him. The punishment for sin, from Adam to the end of eternity, was played out under those olive trees. Time was frozen as everything came down to one transaction that took only minutes to accomplish. Judas was to betray the Son of God.

Jesus spoke of this betrayal at the Last Supper. His words were carefully chosen directly from the 41st Psalm. His task was now accomplished in teaching a handful of men what would change the entire world. The final straw had to be put into motion by Judas so that this one prophetic scripture in Psalm 41 could be played out. As they sat around the table in this critical moment, He says:

(Jesus speaking) "I know whom I have chosen; but that the Scripture may be fulfilled, 'He who eats bread with Me has lifted up his heel against Me."

John 13:18 and Psalm 41:9

Do you see it? This proves how vital Psalm 41 is. If we read it like a flowery, poetic song that David sang overlooking his sheep, we will miss the mark. If we try to only apply the Psalm to the issues affecting the life of King David at that time, we will lose its power. As well, if we believe what he is writing in Psalm 41 only applies to him, it won't have any impact. If Psalm 41:9 was the doorway to the Son of God to perform His destiny, shouldn't we also apply that same faith and understanding to the rest of the Psalm? If the ransom of every sickness, demonic attack, and damnation itself that could happen from Calvary to eternity was activated in the betrayal by Judas in verse 9 of Psalm 41, then surely, we can apply verse 1, 2 and 3 to what we call a pandemic.

Psalm 41:1-3 was laid out in perfect order to be effective. The very first line should be our target to allow the remaining declarations to counteract any sickness from an endemic, pandemic, or plague no matter what the name or time it enters the population. These small three verses show us where to apply our faith and teach us the authority of that very same faith. The Psalmist writes the words that cause every enemy we have to back away. He makes it noticeably clear that this is effective in this day, and in our time. Even my own story of healing from COVID-19 will prove it. All that is needed is for us to believe. God is the same yesterday, today, and forever, and for such a time as this, He is the One who is bringing revelation into our hearts in this dangerous day we live. Even the Psalm ends in final victory to be declared by our faith.

"Blessed be the Lord God of Israel, from everlasting and to everlasting. Amen and Amen."

Psalm 41:13

## The Roadmap

Not only will I be writing out fresh revelation given to me, but I will also be taking some sections of the previous books to clarify each verse. Picture with me a roadmap that has several intersecting roads as we travel down the interstate. In the end, we will all reach our destination and hopefully allow different stories in my own life to add color to an already beautiful landscape. When we finish, each of us will be refreshed, and faith-filled to take on any virus the world says will harm us. My very own testimony of healing will back this up.

Before we move on, let's repeat Psalm 41:1-3. Repeat it several times. This is my declaration before I walk into any crowd of people, whether one or a thousand. I pray that as you understand the power of these three small verses, that faith, even just the size of a tiny mustard seed, you will move mountains, and yes, pandemics too, and have them cast into the sea.

Blessed is he who considers the poor;

the LORD will deliver him in time of trouble.


The LORD will preserve him and keep him alive,

and he will be blessed on the earth;

You will not deliver him to the will of his enemies.


The LORD will strengthen him on his bed of illness;

You will sustain him on his sickbed.


Psalm 41:1-3

# CHAPTER TWO

## Blessed Are Those Who Consider the Poor

I will be honest here; I get nervous using the word "blessed" when I write. This word has been slopped around like wet paint on a wall. As Americans, the word is tossed about loosely in our nation. We certainly don't have it as bad as many other countries around the world. Water runs when we turn the faucet, electricity when we hit the switch, fire when we turn on the stove, fuel when we pull up to the gas pump, heat in the winter and cold in the summer are simply things we take for granted. I rarely hear Americans relating these things as some type of blessing. After all, we think this is why we pay taxes. We expect these things. Usually, I hear people use the word blessed in the "extras," such as a new car for the garage, entitlements for a job well done as we face retirement, a child or grandchild is born, a successful surgery, addition the house, etc. I have seen social media of people saying they are blessed because they found the latest in fashion, tire rims for their truck, or purchased the latest exercise equipment. The list goes on as most of us would nod our heads in approval as these are blessings.

I still have this gnawing in my stomach with the word. Or maybe it is the misappropriation as we sometimes throw it around, like talking about sports or the weather. "How are you today?" we casually ask. "I'm blessed, and you?" When David wrote this Psalm, we could generalize the word blessed and define it as someone who has attained something that makes them joyful. One definition of the word blessed actually means "be happy." Indeed, if we escaped being sick by the Coronavirus, we can declare, "we are blessed."

## Consider Consider

When we read the word "consider" in verse one of Psalm 41, most of us would quickly define it as something to think about. However, if we stop there, we will miss the entire length and breadth of what David is saying. It would be like a small trickle of water coming out of the sand in the middle of a desert. Sure, we would consider ourselves to be satisfied if it would quench our parched throats. The small sips of water could be something to make us very happy in such an arid environment. Or we could stand in the middle of a desert and suddenly come upon Niagara Falls, where there would be a constant supply of cold water for us. Now THAT is the difference of what I mean by considering consider.

King David is giving us a key to the kingdom here. He uses the Hebrew word *sakal* for the description of consider. In its basic definition, it means "to look at," much like the trickle of water in the desert example. But the word is implying so much more. To look at something is just the beginning of the definition. The full meaning is to look at something - then investigate it with your mind – then move to the conclusion of attending to it. It is more than just a word but also a process.

That process brings the activation of power. Not only a release of that power going forward but also looks back to the one who is doing the considering. The supernatural going into our yesterdays and tomorrows all at the same time as we consider the poor. Picture this: It is like running the Boston Marathon while holding a mirror. Not only is there power to run forward towards the finish line, but also looking behind you as all the distractions become smaller and smaller. The process builds upon itself with every step towards victory. The definition implies "to become intelligent, prudent and wise so that they will find maturity of understanding or judgment" towards the poor. Let me repeat it all this way:

"Blessed are those who intelligently, prudently, and wisely, with the maturity of understanding and judgment, see a need, and then looking at the complex situation surrounding it, think through how they could best, most intelligently, and wisely bring about a successful solution to it."

Why would David use such a powerful Hebraic word to define how we are to contemplate the word "consider" when thinking of the poor? After all, in his day, he would have seen many poor people around him. We all, at some point, come across the poor and weak. Jesus even said we will always have the poor among us. (John 12:8) Most of us have witnessed people with relative levels of need. It seems to take too much energy analyzing every event that includes the poor in such dramatic terms. Why make such a fuss?

Why? Because the next three verses all point to what God will do for you if you consider the poor. Just look at today's headlines on COVID-19 and then read these three verses. You will quickly see that it's not the poor only that are at risk, but it is you. You're in the same boat with everyone else regarding an unseen virus moving through our neighborhoods. To apply our faith is to use our authority and power that the Holy Spirit gives us. Jesus said it this way:

"Blessed are the merciful, for they shall receive mercy."

Matthew 5:7

Trust me, my friends, when things like pandemics show up, we will need the benefits of being believers in Jesus Christ. If we are believers, then be one whose action points to the genuine benefits He entrusts to us. The next few verses of Psalm 41 prove it. If we put all our faith in putting on a mask to cover our mouth, washing our hands, and standing 6 feet away from each other to keep us protected, we put ourselves in a precarious position. At a time like this, we need power, and Psalm 41 gives us that power. In Jesus name of course.

## Give And It Shall Be Taken

When I speak of the latest news headlines, I sadly also read the stories of ministers, ministries, and organizations that have twisted their message, all in the idea of donors being "blessed." Some use the scripture in Luke 6:38; "Give, and it will be given to you." They will tell you that whatever you give, you will automatically get back and get back even more abundantly. Without getting into a discussion on whether this is right or wrong, we must apply our faith for anything. Many who support our ministry have asked me to agree with them on this principle as they give, and we have seen incredible things happen. But I always teach people that in every decision, we need to put Jesus right smack dab in the middle, not our carnal pleasures wrapped in false teachings.

"But you shall remember the Lord your God, for it is He who gives you power to get wealth, that He may establish His covenant which He swore to your fathers, as it is this day."

Deuteronomy 8:18

If we can orient our prayer that way, then I say, "Yes and Amen." The blessing that comes to us is about His kingdom being established, not your own. The Bible does teach us to sow seeds to grow a harvest. But that seed must be planted in good soil. If we flippantly give every time the person on television asks, the only result will be an empty bank account. Let's be honest; if our returns were automatic every single time we donated, our fingers would be numb by writing checks to ministries all day long.

## My Friend Lloyd

There is an early morning program that seems to portray this so well to anyone watching. On every single show (and I do mean every single one) there are different speakers who will talk about sowing a financial seed to get a financial harvest. They explain being blessed in such down-to-earth terms that it makes me warm and fuzzy inside. It is like my best friend telling me that heaven is ready to open right then for my blessing. Then comes his appeal for someone to have access to that kind of benefit. "If 1000 people would get to their phones right now and give $1000, they too can be a part of this beautiful blessing." As I think about how that seems to make sense from the verses they mentioned, there is a knot inside my belly that holds me back from picking up the phone. But they know this, and the appeal is just getting ramped up. This process in accessing this blessing has been polished so many times, day after day, that it flows from the speaker naturally. The camera slowly zooms in as story after story was told on how normal, hard-working people have jumped on the bandwagon of this blessing. Their bank accounts never stop being replenished from their new "blessed" lifestyle. After all, who wouldn't want that?

I know one of my best friends sure did. My friend Lloyd would do just about anything for anyone. Albeit his walk with the Lord had times of being a little quirky, he loved the Lord and was always ready to serve. Lloyd also had diabetes. He didn't want to talk about it much, but he told me when it was time for him to get an insulin shot, he needed to do it quickly. I also knew that Lloyd didn't have a steady job or income. He was skilled in a little bit of everything as a Jack-Of-All-Trades.

Some weeks he was busy on a project, and some not. One thing for sure, Llyod was an essential part of our life, and we helped him the best we could. Many times, it was he who would get a good-paying project and turn around and be the one to bless us. As we all put Jesus in the middle of our relationship, it was as if he was a family member, or as they say, "a brother from another mother." When things were slow with work, he would watch a program from a ministry that would encourage people to give to receive a blessing. Again, I'm not 100% opposed to that as there is much truth to what the Bible says about prosperity. Where it rubs me wrong is that we have to "buy into" *that* specific ministry to be blessed. They launch campaigns, give titles, and preach sermons that offer different financial and material blessings available to the viewer. It continued day after day, show after show.

One day Lloyd came to me and said he was going shopping for a new Mercedes Benz SUV. That was so entirely out of his league and character that I had to question it. He told me about the most recent show where the evangelist stated that if people were watching his show and needed a new car, the giver would be blessed if they gave sacrificially. Lloyd ended up calling the 1-800 number and gave every single dime from his savings account, about $1500. He was able to speak to the evangelist himself and explained his need for a vehicle. The response was that whatever kind of car he needed, God would bless him with it. Lloyd specifically asked, "Do you mean like a Mercedes Benz?" "Sure! Why not!" was the response. "Whatever car you want, you can have by sowing a sacrificial seed into this ministry." So, they both agreed a Mercedes Benz would be about the best. I think I would agree, that would be one great car. Lloyd was instructed to go directly to the dealership and pick one out and take it for a test drive, which he did. When asked if he were ready to buy it, he told the salesperson he would do that as soon as the blessing came. He was directed to exercise his faith and attempt to take out an insurance policy on that new Mercedes Benz that he didn't even have, to the puzzlement of the insurance agent.

Days turned into weeks with no Mercedes Benz in the driveway. He called the ministry again to confirm that he was doing right to receive his blessing. He was told that maybe he was in error and should look for a vehicle *like* a Mercedes Benz and that perhaps the Lord was saying it was supposed to be a BMW. The voice at the end of the phone encouraged him to hurry to the BMW dealership and get his new vehicle. Again, with the same results…nothing. A third time he called the ministry, and they explained that he didn't have enough faith and needed to give another donation to increase his commitment. The problem was, he was out of money and struggling to make ends meet.

Agreed, Lloyd wasn't the most educated person, but he wasn't stupid either. The realization was setting in that the "blessing" the prosperity preacher offered wasn't going to happen. He even asked for his money back, which you and I know wasn't an option. To make a long story short, and very tragic, Lloyd soon passed away alone from a diabetic coma because he could not afford the medicine he needed. Nobody even noticed except for the mail piling up in his mailbox. Days later, the police made entrance to his house and found Lloyd dead. I share this story as it touches a nerve in me. My friend was promised a blessing, told the blessing was coming, and passed away waiting for that blessing to appear.

I assume we all have some type of story that we relate to as being "blessed." I don't want to get too far off the subject. I need to stay on target as to what the Holy Spirit was teaching me about the virus outbreak. When we intelligently, prudently, or wisely, with the maturity of understanding and judgment, see a need, and then looking at the complex situation surrounding it, think through how we could best, most intelligently, and wisely bring about a successful solution to it, then we will see the results of that consideration.

## Who Are The Poor?

Working in the nation of Haiti for the better part of 20 years has given me much understanding of "the poor." I run the risk of painting a picture of poverty that you may not identify with. I'm not here to tell you how grim poverty can be. We have all seen the television commercials on late-night TV showing the sick and dying in some faraway continent. I don't minimize that, and I understand that more than most. To see the agony of body and soul from starvation is no small thing. To be handed sick children who would later die all because there was no availability to the simplest of medical care can frustrate anyone's thinking. I must fight that every day in the line of work that I do. I must also consider the poor when I try to come up with solutions that work in our area.

I'm also not here to politicize poverty. Part of my job as a missionary is to find resources to help us care for the poor in Haiti. Some people that I ask for support come at me as if I am blind to poverty in the USA. "Don't you know we have poor people here." some strongly retort. "My money goes to poverty in my backyard before any other country than ours." If I've heard it once, I have heard it repeated a hundred times. I agree that everyone has the right to make their decision. But instead of trying to convince someone of how poor a child may be in the mountains of Haiti, I simply agree and make them a challenge. I invite them to come to Haiti and see for themselves that kind of poverty. If they still think that the misery of a western nation is the same as a developing country like Haiti, then they won, and I will concede. I won't ever bother them again about it. As you may have guessed, nobody has taken me up on the offer. Generally, when people want to argue the poverty levels, they probably don't consider the poor at all, whether here or there. However, coming from someone who lives part of their life in a developing nation, especially an area struck by dire poverty, I can testify; there is a difference.

Take for example, what we see at food banks in America during this pandemic. In every large city, the line of cars to get food can go for miles around the distribution area. There probably is little doubt that these people are in need, yet they may not be poor. If you look closely at the line of cars, it seems like a new car dealership. Sure, there might be the occasional older model "clunkers" that people in need can only afford, but for the most part, it is one newer car, truck, and SUV after another and another. All are in line to get food into their kitchen. Indeed, their situation changed with this pandemic, and they are in desperate need of food. I'm not minimizing that. This crisis causes a new level of poor in America, but this isn't the poverty that I'm describing.

I recently read an article that told of a business owner who owned several houses that she rented for vacationers. When the Coronavirus was spreading in the United States, and equally spreading in the media, she lost all the short-term renters she had lined up for all her beachfront properties. Now the mortgage is due on them, and she has no income to pay it. She stood in the front yard of a very pricey rental and exclaimed, "I must have made a deal with the devil." No, as desperate as that sounds, that also isn't the kind of poor I'm talking about.

I can still feel the punch in my gut as I saw the news story of the widow that lost her husband of 62 years to COVID-19. Because of social distancing, she was the only person allowed at the burial. Not only was she lamenting the loss of her long-time partner, but her thoughts were equally on her financial situation. She shook her head and wondered how she would go on financially without his Social Security check each month. I thought to myself how tragic this was that she had to think about finances in her grieving time. Nope, this also isn't the poor I'm speaking of.

There are so many heart-wrenching stories of what first responders encountered when the virus was taking so many lives. The news spoke about a nurse who had to walk away from her job because the hospital couldn't guarantee the proper protection equipment she needed to stay healthy. She was in agony about her decision. She explained how she planned on her stimulus check from the government to get her through. Her fears compounded as the check wasn't received yet. As despairing and unfair as this sounds, and no doubt it can be much worse as the wheels of government turn slowly, this also isn't the poor I have seen.

Certainly, I'm not talking about the ministry to which my friend Lloyd gave all his savings. I can't judge someone's heart; only God does that. But one peek on the internet of the millions of dollars that some organizations bring into their glass buildings is also not the poverty I'm describing. Even if they show poor, naked, and hungry children on their television programs, it is not the same.

These dreadful examples of lives that have been forever altered from this pandemic aren't the picture that I want to paint about the poor. Each of these examples has a fallback plan; usually, the United States government or, possibly, family or friends who can work at jobs deemed essential. As agonizing as these and many other stories can be, this still isn't the poor that Psalm 41 speaks of. Let me explain.

## Enter Dana

After several years of being a missionary, I started to feel comfortable in my surroundings. The ministry was moving forward. God added the right people to our lives. Finances were beginning to come in regularly. Intercessors were praying for us daily. So, all in all, we were humming along like a well-oiled machine. I guess that should have been somewhat expected for growing ministries that are starting to reach the harvest. Nevertheless, things can go 180 degrees in the opposite direction very quickly in Haiti.

In 2002 I had a cousin from Ohio visit us. He had seen poverty in developing countries before, but nothing on the scale of Haiti. It seemed that every village softened his heart more and more.

As we turned the corner to walk from the village to our house, I was interrupted by a woman I have known for a few years. Her name was Vercilee, and she has eight children from eight different men. Naturally, she was destitute, and the children were always near starvation. I usually made it a priority that when I was near her house, I would stop by if I had the resources to help. I can promise you that I use the term "house" very loosely. It was made of old pieces of discarded sheet metal tied to tree branches that were burrowed into the mud floor. Because she sold cooking charcoal for a living, the inside, including the children, were always covered in black charcoal dust. Due to the sheet metal being so rusted, the house was constantly damp from the tropical rains. Some of the larger openings were covered in cardboard, which allowed some rain to run off away from their one bed, albeit temporarily. When the hot sun would come out, beams of light would permeate the darkness from the many circular holes that used to have a nail driven through them before it was discarded to the trash heap. Some days it looked like a disco dance hall as the sunbeams of bright light would shine through the charcoal dust and humidity inside.

You could tell the terrible conditions had deeply touched my cousin. As he began asking me how I coped with so many impoverished people, I explained that there are the poor, and then there are the *really* poor. Vercilee indeed fell into the really poor category. He asked me how he could best help her. The obvious answer was to get her and the children out of a house made of sheet metal.

However, before moving forward, there needed to be a conversation with her about her responsibility to the eight children she currently had. She needed to stop falling into the same trap of trusting a man who promised to take care of her and her kids, only to have him leave as soon as she ended up pregnant. It was essential not to come off sounding like we were forcing her to do something to receive help. She needed to understand God's blessing. The Bible teaches that there are decisions we make in our lives that God simply cannot bless. It doesn't change His love for her, but the continual cycle of having another man's baby every other year wasn't the answer. I shared with her some stories from the Bible and certain scriptures. She was not offended and welcomed my advice based on the Word of God.

I knew that my cousin wanted to help her get into a proper house, but I needed some time to see if there was a real change in her life. If I could not see a modification, we would merely be making the problem worse as we rewarded someone for bad behavior. In these villages, everyone is watching, even when you think your actions are private. Most of the villagers were just as poverty-stricken as she was.

Following our conversation, she would walk from her village to church every Sunday and Wednesday, with all the kids in tow. Not only that, but she came with a smile on her face and sincerely wanted to help serve in the church. Her rededication to Christ was genuine, and even though I would make it a point to greet her and the kids, she never asked me for anything.

After a few months had passed, I gave my cousin a call and told him about my plan to rent her a concrete house. He was so enthusiastic that he sent enough finances to rent a home for a year and for several bags of food to be delivered at random dates.

I need to pause here as I know most of my readers have been raised in western culture. When I mention a house to Americans, we often picture what we see all around us. That is not the same in Haiti. In Haiti, a home is generally one 16x16 room with a porch for cooking. No Living Room, Master Bedroom, Dining Room, Bathroom, Kitchen, etc., like we think of here in the United States. The house we rented for her had strong concrete walls with two cement blocks turned sideways as windows, a concrete floor, and a roof that didn't leak every time it rained. The front door was made of plywood with a padlock clasp to keep people from stealing from her. To many of us, we would wonder if we could even live in a place like that. I have seen American bathrooms bigger than this house, but to her, it was a palace, even with eight children.

It was such a joy to be able to take food to her. My cousin felt that it was his responsibility to adopt this family. Several times one of them needed to see a doctor, and the expenses were taken care of. I would always make it a point to remind her that this all came to be from her faithfulness to follow God and become the kind of mother her children would respect. Even in a harsh environment like Haiti, her self-esteem soared. It is hard to express how great it was when I came across women who were in the same predicament as she was and found that it was not me ministering to them, but Vercilee. She was able to do it in a way that could never be received from a foreigner.

As can happen, many times too frequently, a major disaster strikes Haiti. On February 13, 2010, a 7.0 earthquake destroyed Port-Au-Prince. Death and destruction were everywhere. To this day, nobody knows how many lives were lost. Some are forever entombed in buildings that now lay in waste. During this disaster, children who lost families instantly became orphans.

Since the village of Titanyen is the first village traveling north out of Port-Au-Prince on a major roadway, it became a natural place to bring lost children. As a missionary, the information I was hearing was that if people brought the orphans to Titanyen, maybe, just maybe, somebody would pick them up. As terrible as that sounds, it was a better option than an almost certain death that awaited them in the city. Along with dealing with their destruction, the village was overwhelmed. The agencies and organizations that were trying to cope with such a massive catastrophe were on overdrive. Stories circulated about these orphaned children dying in the streets. It was a dark time for a nation that had suffered so much already.

Several weeks after the worst of the disaster had passed and people were getting back to some kind of normalcy, I found myself in Titanyen again. My cousin had sent some finances to get food for Vercilee's family, and I had several families to pay my respects to who lost a family member to the earthquake.

As I loaded up the rice bag on my shoulder, I came into the courtyard where Vercilee lived and was shocked to see this poor helpless child. In a world of sick and starving children, she certainly was one of the worst cases I had seen. My daughter Laura was with me that day and immediately went to the child, who didn't budge. When they see a white person, most Haitian children have some type of expression, whether good or bad. But this little girl was so weak, she simply just stared with these big, black eyes. That wasn't the only thing that was big on her. Out of this frail skinny little beanpole of a body protruded a substantial bloated belly. A sure sign that she was in the process of starvation. To this day, I have never seen a frown that was so evident that it pulled on her cheekbones. We were even afraid to pick her up because she looked like she would break apart right in our very arms.

My daughter quickly opened her backpack to find a protein bar or snack that she could give her. We were interrupted promptly by Vercilee, who explained that the food could harm her. She was in such a state of starvation that only small amounts of powdered milk and simple bread could be given to her. She then told us she was out of food and hoping that we would come to her house. She never knew when I would be in her village, so she asked God to "steer" me off the highway and to her home that day. Little did she know I was coming to her with bags of food anyway. She broke out in singing a song and praising God for hearing her prayer. After I brought in the food, the questions began to flood from our minds to our mouths. Who is this poor girl? Where did she come from? Why is she starving? What is her story?

After a few minutes of discussion, we found out that she was an orphan from the earthquake. That is as close of an answer we could get since she just showed up lying on the ground by the highway. The next logical question came from my mouth to this very grave situation: "Who is taking care of this little girl"?

The next few moments could be one of the most embarrassing moments of my Christian life and certainly, as a pastor and a missionary. Again, as an American, much like many of you reading this, my western culture speaks to me subconsciously. I thought that surely there has to be an agency, organization, or government assistance of some kind that should be contacted to assist such a helpless girl teetering on the verge of death from starvation.

I could feel my blood pressure rising as my jaw was dropping. I couldn't believe the answer Vercilee gave me. "Well, Pastor Don, this is Dana; I am taking her in," she said nervously.

"What!?!" I said as I threw back my cape over my shoulder so that everyone could see the Superman "S" on my shirt. My hands then rested on each side of my hips as I stuck my chest out. I could sense my missionary superpowers shining down from heaven on me as the warm breeze of blessing rustled through my hair. Being such a great man of compassion and power, I opened my mouth…

…Oh, how I wish I had never let the next few statements come from my lips. Over just about 60 seconds, Jesus brought out His pruning shears and began to chop. The more I spoke on my knowledge of the poor, the deeper the pruning.

"Vercilee, you can't even take care of the children you have," I retorted. "Without me bringing you food, the kids wouldn't even be able to eat today." Then came the perfect setup in my self-pride and arrogance. "If you can't even take care of your own children, do you think it is wise to bring another child into your house?"

Over the next few moments, I went from Superman to a monkey. I was so humiliated and embarrassed that even today, I never get away from her response. Each word from my translator made me shrink smaller and smaller. "Oh, but Pastor Don. I used to live in a sheet-metal house." "Yes, I remember," I responded. "But now I live in a house made of cement," she said as she smacked the dirty wall made of concrete. As she raised her hands to heaven, she reiterated, "A cement house!" She continued as my humiliation began to rise, and my superiority began to sink. "Because I live in a concrete house, I made a vow to God that whoever I encounter that I can help, I am going to." Ever so slowly, I began to look at her tiny one-room house as she told me in great detail the day she walked to the market, and there sat this little girl in the mud. She watched as people would walk behind, in front of, and over top of the little girl. She then told me again, as if I didn't hear the first time, "I made a vow to God to help the next person I see. But not just anyone. I made a vow to help anyone who was as poor as me." Here is the poor, considering the poor.

I guess the tears that began to roll down my cheeks were enough for her to quit talking about how blessed she was with her concrete home. At that very moment, when my eyes went down to meet the face of this dirty, hungry, lost, little girl, everyone could sense the Master Gardener was making his cuts in my heart. Somehow, I missed the seriousness of this child. She was so close to death that she didn't even have the energy to cry. In that instant, my tears made up for it. I believe Jesus says it best in the gospel of Luke:

"A man was going down from Jerusalem to Jericho when he was attacked by robbers. They beat him, leaving him half dead. A priest happened to be going down the same road passed by on the other side. So too, a Levite saw him and passed by. But a Samaritan came where the man was, and when he saw him, he took pity on him. He went to him and bandaged his wounds..."

Luke 10:30-35 (edits mine)

Then came the question Jesus asks in the next verse, which was what the Holy Spirit was asking me as the pruning process continued.

"Which of these three do you think was a neighbor to the man who fell into the hands of robbers?"

Luke 10:36

Going back to our definition of consider, let me change this question a little as we reflect on Psalm 41. Which of the people intelligently, prudently, or wisely, with maturity of understanding and judgment, saw a need, and then looks at the complex situation surrounding it, thinks through how he could best, most intelligently, and wisely bring about a successful solution to it? That precisely explains what the Samaritan did. He not only considered the poor and weak, but he also came up with the answer to the problem. In the light of talking about Psalm 41:1, The Adamson Version would ask, "Which of the poor should we choose for our consideration?"

How incredibly foolish I felt at that moment. You would have thought that all my years of doing ministry, helping children, and loving people, I would have discerned a little bit about why this young girl was there that day. Her dire condition of poverty should have been a sign that I needed to think deeper into why she was there, but with the increased activity of helping people after the earthquake, I was on an auto-pilot mode as we dealt with the new challenges we faced. Our area's desperation was drastic, but we were meeting the needs of people, and the ministry was moving forward. In summary, I became very "comfortable" in the disaster relief mode in which I found myself. Too comfortable to stop looking at the 99 to see the 1.

## Consider The Poor

Now finally, that is the type of poor I am talking about. The word in the original language from Psalm 41:1 means; poor, needy, weak, lean, all of which described the little girl Dana, and hundreds of others just like her that we see in the mountains of Haiti. These are the undesirables. Those who can't help themselves. The ones in which the world sees no value.

I cannot stress this enough. There is such a doorway to power in the first line of verse one, and I would line it up to be used against a pandemic going around the globe. This verse is the entrance to the works of Calvary to start being effective in our lives. It is the answer when I stand at the front doors of a grocery store, not knowing who may be infected inside. It simply unties the bondage that a pandemic or plague can bring to us, emotionally, physically, financially, relationally, spiritually, even reaching the next generation who will follow us. As well, we will learn later in the book; it does affect our eternity. How I apply Psalm 41:1 isn't just about me, but my children and children's children. It is like a faucet that is ready to release heaven's answer to a virus that seems to know no bounds. But instead of volumes of benefits that would take many pages to explain, it is all contained in just two verses following. As I have stated, if we will do verse 1, then verses 2 and 3 will be more active in our lives than the fear that the news tells us we should have.

The New Testament makes this so clear through the Apostle Paul's letters. It wasn't just a one-time act, but something that always weighed on his mind. Not just him only, but considering the poor was woven throughout all the Apostles. In Galatians, Paul speaks of the time he went to Jerusalem to meets with the "pillars of the church," Peter, James, and John. Once they understood the grace of God was being poured out to the Gentiles as well as the Jews, they sent Paul with this instruction.

"They desired only that we should remember the poor, the very thing which I also was eager to do."

Galatians 2:10

Can you see it? After their discussions in the spiritual, those who walked with Jesus when He was on the earth gave only one request in the natural. That is to consider the poor. Could the Holy Spirit be guiding them because of the hardships that would be in front of Paul? Difficulties that only God would know. If God is not a respecter of persons, then He had to provide a key that would be needed to unlock the doors of adversity that Paul would face. Psalm 41 is like a silver lining in a cloud, as Paul explained his hardships this way:

"Are they servants of Christ? I know I sound like a madman, but I have served him far more! I have worked harder, been put in prison more often, been whipped times without number, and faced death again and again. Five different times the Jewish leaders gave me thirty-nine lashes. Three times I was beaten with rods. Once I was stoned. Three times I was shipwrecked. Once I spent a whole night and a day adrift at sea. I have traveled on many long journeys. I have faced danger from rivers and from robbers. I have faced danger from my own people, the Jews, as well as from the Gentiles. I have faced danger in the cities, in the deserts, and on the seas. And I have faced danger from men who claim to be believers but are not. I have worked hard and long, enduring many sleepless nights. I have been hungry and thirsty and have often gone without food. I have shivered in the cold, without enough clothing to keep me warm. Then, besides all this, I have the daily burden of my concern for all the churches."

2 Corinthians 11:23-28

What a list! If you are like me, you would wonder how did he escape from so much adversity and live to tell about it? By his testimony, we know that Psalm 41 was deeply ingrained in his heart and mind because of Paul's lineage and training. If anyone there was that knew that power that comes from considering the poor, it was the Apostle Paul. There is another list Paul gives us. It is a list of his qualification in following the law.

"I was circumcised when I was eight days old. I am a pure-blooded citizen of Israel and a member of the tribe of Benjamin—a real Hebrew if there ever was one! I was a member of the Pharisees, who demand the strictest obedience to the Jewish law."

Philippians 3:5

I must ask myself how many times did Psalm 41 make an impact on Paul's decisions? As the storms were raging all around him, could he of invoked the power and promise of Psalm 41:1-3, all because he considered the poor? I feel like I go through the same principles today as I leave the safety of my home, wondering if the hardship of a deadly virus is waiting for me out in the world. Instead of putting all my hope into a fabric mask, I focus on Psalm 41. If fear wants to attempt to control me, I recite the power promises that come with considering the poor.

## Lessons In The Middle

If you know me and what I do in the world, you could probably call "foul" because of my position. After all, it isn't fair since what I do for a living sets me up to consider the poor easily. The calling from God will not let me get very far away from always thinking about the Haitians that are a part of my life. My staff, teachers, security, custodians, drivers, and many others who work without a title are vital. Most get a monthly check, some get paid per project, and still, others volunteer. I try to do something for everyone.

We had a celebration after the end of school last year. When I walked into the room to give everyone encouragement, I could barely get in the door. There were 64 people jammed into that conference room. I asked my Haitian Director, "Who are all these people?" He just shook his head and laughed and said they were all my employees. The word "employees" is too cold a description. These people are family: The Acts 29 family. Being responsible for all these people can bring stress, as you can imagine. As the 20th of each month approaches, I can feel the pressure start to build as I anticipate payroll, which comes at the end of each month. In 2013 my entire staff consisted of 3 men and a pickup truck, which made payroll a lot easier. As the days tick closer to the end of the month, I will often check the bank account. That pressure is genuine. So yes, I must consider the poor every day of my life. That doesn't give me extra points regarding Psalm 41:1. It is almost the opposite. I can't just "consider them" with warm sunshine and butterflies filling my soul.

On top of that, I need to decide what part of the budget goes towards projects that will help pull people out of poverty, such as agriculture, water collection, or sanitation projects. All of them require finances to accomplish. That adds another layer of responsibility as undoubtedly many will benefit from these projects. Take that information and add it to what I'm talking about in this book, a pandemic that affects everyone *and their jobs*…including those who support ministries like ours. I can promise it will surely stretch your commitments towards considering the poor.

How do I do it? I must approach it by faith, just like you do. I must believe in Psalm 41:1 that tells me I will be blessed if I consider the poor. The Adamson Version says, "relieved are those who bear in mind all the Haitian employees." I'm not trying to "market" our poor. The 10,000% growth we have seen isn't just vision casting or future hopes of the ministry; it is real numbers from 2013-2019! Many are depending on me. As well, I depend on others whose livelihoods could be changed through a tiny virus. Let me make it raw: if I don't pay, they don't eat. So, it isn't as if I'm skipping down the sidewalk of ease, teasing those that I pass by about an extra advantage I have in considering the poor. The consideration comes with much sweat and tears. Therefore, my prayer life points forward to those I support and backward towards those who helped us get that support. Either direction, it is always centered around Psalm 41. I can apply my faith to these specific promises for those that come alongside us.

## Bringing It Home

Let me bring this important chapter to a close. In the middle of the fear that this virus was invading every corner of our nation, my 1-year old grandson needed to go to the hospital.

He put something into his mouth, and no one was sure if he ate it, swallowed it, or hopefully spit it out. Only a trip to the emergency room would tell us. My son called me and asked me to pray. His concern was not the immediate situation alone. But hospitals were mentioned in every type of media about being a source for the Coronavirus spread. Of course, I told him I would pray, but I have something far more effective than praying what I hope the resolution could be. I have the promise of three little verses in Psalm 41 to be released and to start working on my behalf for my son and grandson.

Let me add more pressure to this already alarming situation. My son said the people in the emergency room were all quite annoyed and short-tempered and acted as if he was a bad parent for not watching his son all 1440 minutes of the day. Maybe the staff was stretched thin, possibly some of their co-workers had contracted the virus, or perhaps they were just in a bad mood as the news wasn't too cheerful those days. I don't know why they were so coldhearted to my son. I gave him these instructions: "you take care of my grandson and let me take care of mean people through prayer." I can say that because I have a promise. If I consider the poor, I have a signed contract by the Lord that I have power over adverse situations. Of course, the will of God is that people wouldn't be mean. I didn't have to approach the situation as if I lumped everything into being in or out of the will of God. No, I had a promise to remind Him. In my life, the poor were considered, and now I needed Him to move in this situation according to that promise.

In the end, it worked just as it was supposed to, and all was well. Did Psalm 41 fix the problem by supernaturally dissolving what he may have ingested, or was it all for nothing because he didn't swallow anything in the first place? From my position, a thousand miles away, I don't know or care. The result was that I received a good report, and even the hospital staff became nicer. My efforts and energy weren't ultra-focused on the hospital circumstances surrounding my grandson. My focus was on the promise of Psalm 41 to help me in the crisis.

Take a breath now. We are going to get to the good stuff! Let's recite these one more time before moving to the promises.

Blessed are those who consider the poor;
the Lord will deliver them in the day of trouble.
The Lord will preserve them and keep them alive,
and they will be blessed on the earth,
and You will not deliver them to the will of their
enemies.
The Lord will sustain them on the sickbed;
You will restore all his lying down in his illness.

Psalm 41:1-3 (paraphrase mine)

# CHAPTER THREE

## The LORD Will Deliver
## Them In The Day Of Trouble.

I can testify with many other missionaries in Haiti that the country can hurt you. But as well, the Haitian people are some of the most exceptional people you will ever meet. The nation itself has so much beauty to offer. It is their identification and agreement to superstition and voodoo worship that can bring painful results for anyone trying to make progress. Sometimes the only way to fully understand how God delivers us from trouble is that we must be in the thick of that trouble. Only then can you shout when the victory comes. We can all testify, no matter what country we are in, afflictions come to us all. It is our faith in God and how we orient our faith that makes the difference.

While I was having one of the darkest times of my life in Haiti, there was a prophet from Ghana, West Africa, praying. It was as if he picked up a radio signal out of heaven concerning what was happening to me. Through a divine connection, he was introduced to my pastor in Dayton, Ohio. A particular Friday night church service was given to the prophet in our Ohio church. As the service was underway, the prophet told my pastor how the evil spirits strategized to take my life in Haiti. He explained that God showed him the attacks planned against me, and together he and my home church community prayed and stopped the attack. How incredible! All the while, I had no clue about what was happening. How much more can I declare, "Blessed are those who consider the poor; the Lord will deliver them in the day of trouble!"? Read on, and you will understand.

With some slight editing due to poor recording, mispronunciations of English, and to save time, here is what the prophet said. (please email me at don@acts29missions.org if you are interested in hearing the live recording)

## Deliverance From Big Trouble

Prophet: "God has an assignment for this church in Haiti. The Lord is in this place. But the devil is trying to undermine it. I am talking about one of your sons. You have a pastor by the name of Don. Don? [He never met me or knew anything about me]. Don…where is he?"

Senior Pastor: "He is in Haiti."

Prophet: "What is he doing there?"

Senior Pastor: "He is a missionary."

Prophet: "The devil wants to kill him. To undermine what God wants to do. The devil is a liar. Whenever God tries to do a new thing, the devil always tries to interfere and bring destruction and undermine what God wants to do. That is why in the scriptures, whenever a new deliverer is born, the enemy would dispatch his demons to go after the deliverer. I believe the devil really wants to go after him, but I believe God today that the devil is a liar. The Lord is telling me that where he is, there is a lot of witchcraft oppression, and that in the vicinity in which he is in, there are four witchcraft strongholds. God is telling me that there is a conspiracy by the witches of that vicinity, that he is disturbing them. They want to plan an accident against him. Is he married? Is he there with the wife? (My wife just arrived back in Ohio the night before.) It was like the wife had received a call that the husband was involved in an accident in Haiti. And the thing affected the church, and it hurt you so bad and undermined the edge, the joy, to go over there and work. The devil wants to hurt this church. But the devil is a liar. I reject the plan of the enemy."

At this point, several pastors and leaders came forward to pray for me. During that prayer, the prophet spoke up again, "I saw the casket spiritually being brought into this church. And the Lord told me that it is his casket. But if it is the plan of the enemy, the devil is a liar. The devil cannot undermine what God wants to do in that nation. And in that nation, he cannot hurt you. Whenever he really wants to hurt you as a believer, he goes for your feelings. And when your feelings are hurt, it affects your effectiveness. When the enemy really wants to attack the man in person, the Bible says, they cried until they had no power in them. For the Bible (declares) when you grieve in your souls, the enemy will attack your soul. Your soul is your emotion, will, intellect. So, whenever the devil attacks your soul, it affects everything you do. You see, the devil wants to get in there and affect someone that is so close to the mission and to what God wants to do. But the devil is a liar. I want you to call the fire of God to devour the country and the witches in that vicinity. We are declaring that they shall die one by one. For the GLORY OF THE LORD! Somebody say 'fire, fire, fire.' We intercede for him. He said his covenant is secured. Hallelujah. Amen. Thank you very much. If all of you can fast for him tomorrow, I would fully appreciate it. Let us lift him up to God. The Bible says to be each brother's keeper. Let's hold hands and pray and declare his life is secure in the blood of the Lamb, that by the powers of heaven and the influence of Yeshua and the God of the Armies of Israel we declare that his life is secured and safe. He shall live to accomplish his mission on earth. Not until he has finished it, heaven shall not receive him. Somebody give the Lord a hand of praise."

## The Darkness Was Gone!

You can imagine the correspondence I got from the United States the next morning as they told me what this prophet said. I remember listening and reading what people were saying to me about this attack. Even though I attempted to explain what I was feeling, most were clueless about it until the Holy Spirit revealed it. The core of this supernatural message wasn't all about me but about how the people had the power to pray and stop what Satan meant for harm against me. Believers that were a thousand miles away in Ohio were changing the outcome of my life in Haiti. In one accord, they were committed to God's liberation for me.

This event was a divine deliverance from trouble. It was a war that was happening around me, yet I couldn't see. It isn't much different than my faith in a God that I can't see either, yet, one brought torment and the other peace. Most of those pastors that prayed for me financially supported our work in Haiti. Therefore, when they were praying, they had the right to invoke Psalm 41 because of the promise. As they considered the poor (our vision and ministry in Haiti), God would hear their prayers, and deliverance came. The commitment and the power that came with it were displayed. Countless lives have been changed because God promised that He would deliver us from trouble.

We know that voodoo temples and shopping malls are quite different, yet there is also a very similar risk these days. Witchcraft on one side and a virus on the other, both are wanting to bring destruction. As I walk into a grocery store, restaurant, or hardware business, I must ask myself, "Is there a threat to me in that place?" My job is to breathe the air, not to analyze it for viruses. The scientists in the media answer my questions as "yes, there is a threat anywhere I go." But I have something from heaven protecting me that trumps their scientific predictions on this planet. Jesus declares that heaven and earth will pass away, but this line of scripture is my promise from God and will never pass away.

"The Lord will deliver them [me] in the day of trouble."
Psalm 41:1b

How much more trouble could there be than an invisible virus that has shut down many parts of the world? So many millions of lives are now at risk. The entire future of generations now seems to be sinking in quicksand. Families separated from burials. Weddings canceled. Retirement packages evaporated overnight. Government policies got put on hold. Technological breakthroughs in medicine set aside to devote all the energies toward finding a cure for the virus. Successful businesses now lay in waste. I could go on and on, but it all points to one thing: trouble. The promise is that He will deliver us in the day of evil so that we can say, "It is well with my soul." When we consider the poor, God said He would deliver us from this calamity. If I stopped right now, we could shout the victory on this promise of God, but the scriptures don't end here in just the first verse. We have even more assurances in the next two verses that deal directly with pandemics. Keep your faith high and keep reading. You, too, will see the plan of God to defeat this foe.

# CHAPTER FOUR

## The Lord Will Preserve Them
## And Keep Them Alive

Who can forget the videos we have seen on the news of the heroic doctors and nurses trying to bring life back to a body that has succumbed to the virus? I can't get out of my mind the nurse frantically performing CPR on a young patient who everyone thought would survive the COVID-19 attack since he was the picture of health. Only time will allow scientists and statisticians to figure out why the virus was more devastating to certain classes of people than others. Maybe there isn't a right answer. It seemed that the first news about this disease was that it was mainly affecting older people. The young and healthy only had to worry about sniffles and sneezes if they caught the virus. Then the reports came out each day of more and more youthful individuals dying from the illness. What agony there must have been on doctors and nurses who had to determine who might live or die.

Even more bewildering than that were the different treatments that worked in some areas yet failed in others. Some patients would take an experimental drug and would completely recover the very next day. As this miracle story came out, governments would spend millions stockpiling the drug, only to later learn that the particular drug was proven to be ineffective in stopping the virus. Like a rollercoaster ride, we saw this happen with many medications or treatments, which seemed to work miracles in some and do nothing in others. Since the person's faith isn't mentioned, could it be that those miraculous stories were coming from believers? Could Psalm 41:2 be actively working in their bodies even more than medicine?

When I read verse 2 that says, "The Lord will preserve them and keep them alive," it puts the connotation that they are in a problem to start. That life-giving preservation may look like an isolated room with ventilators and machines on every side, but the room's details have no power over a promise from God to preserve them. It isn't how you look when He starts this miraculous turnaround, but how He finishes it. His promise ends the same: we are alive.

## Submarine Truck

If you haven't been to a developing country like Haiti, it is challenging to understand our road conditions. Here in the United States, many off-road enthusiasts will pay a fee to take their motorcycles and trucks on these unpaved roads, all for the thrill. Yet, this kind of off-road environment looks like normal road conditions in Haiti's mountains. Rocks, holes, mudslides, washed-out bridges, you name it. When I built the school, we experienced 17 flat tires in 3 days. That should give you an idea of what we face every day we drive those roads. What does all of this have to do with the Lord preserving our lives? Read on.

It was on these kinds of roads that I had to go 9 hours north to a place called Saint-Raphael to pay my respects to the family of a slain politician. This road trip happened during Haiti's rainy season. We had a great deal of experience in crossing swollen rivers, yet we had a serious concern about being in such a remote area in the countryside of Haiti. We found ourselves crossing a river, which was slow-moving with no threat of flooding. However, we still had four or five hours of travel from that location before our return to that same spot. While we were traveling, a tropical thunderstorm developed and turned this same calm river into something deep, wide, and angry- and we had to cross it. In the pitch black of the night, all that I could see were the headlights on the other side of the river as trucks lined up waiting to cross and drivers unsure if their vehicles could withstand the swift-flowing water. To make matters worse, I was not in what I call "my submarine truck." That description is pretty much exactly what I need when crossing rivers. My submarine truck is a heavy Ford F-250 truck that usually had the power and weight to cross raging rivers. The door seals long ago worn away, which helped this kind of large truck sink to the bottom. The river water would flood through the doors on one side and exit out the other, all the while filling up the truck bed too. With all this weight, it allowed the tires to grab the rocks deep in the river, and it never got stuck. (well...rarely, but that is for another book) The submarine truck was much better at navigating the rough terrain and rivers of Haiti than the smaller industrial truck I was driving that night. This smaller truck was practically brand new. Even though it was a 4-wheel drive, it certainly was not made for harsh driving conditions such as crossing an unknown river in a flash flood. As those who know me will confirm, I can become impatient in these situations. That night was no different, as I desperately wanted to get home. We were in the middle of nowhere in Haiti, surrounded by wind, rain, and lightning.

Since I wasn't familiar with this river, I couldn't be sure where the best entrances and exits were. All I knew was that I wasn't going to sit in the wet truck all night waiting for the storm to subside. If this storm ended up being a tropical depression, it could take days for me to be able to cross.

I decided I needed two people outside the truck guiding me. With my staff of three, they drew straws to see which two were going into the river in front of the truck. I reasoned that if I could have them holding my truck bumper, they could communicate to me if there was a big hole or a tree in the water. The two staff members that lost stepped outside and reluctantly took their clothes off down to their underwear. I also asked two local men sitting nearby if I could hire them to help us get across as they were familiar with the area. The idea seemed simple enough to lower the risk factor as I put two men on my left and two on the right.

As we inched into the river, the local people told me to drive left of the usual route because a large, unseen rock had washed down from the storm and was sitting near the exit of the river.

I was nervous as we kept getting farther and farther away from the usual exit where I could detect the other truck headlights. I could see my men being pushed down the river as each one held tightly to the other. When we reached the halfway mark, we had entered the no-turning-back phase. It was all forward, no matter what. I didn't dare try to push in the clutch and downshift to a lower gear. Down-shifting may have helped with traction but would risk us losing momentum. If that happened, we would be at the mercy of a very unmerciful river. The only option was to keep my foot stuck on that gas pedal and watch where my men were telling me to go. I could feel the pressure of the river pushing the truck down as the windshield wipers swished at full speed back and forth, trying to clear a line of sight from the water that was coming over the glass. Between the river water mixing with the pouring down rain, and both headlights underwater, it was almost impossible to see the men. Suddenly, the truck began to lift from the water pressure. Since it was a newer truck and the door seals were still good, they didn't allow much water into the cab. That caused us to start to float like a boat, just the opposite of what my heavy truck does.

You cannot convince me that Psalm 41 isn't real and actively working in situations like that. As my truck was starting to float away and the tires would not grip the bottom of the river, I believed that the Lord would preserve me and keep me alive…even in a flooded river where much larger trucks were unwilling to cross. No, it wasn't a viral pandemic we were facing, but something that was a real threat to our lives.

There was such a great feeling of relief when the men began telling me to sharply turn toward the exit of the river as they could feel we had just made it past the big rock. Victory felt good as the water began receding, and we came out onto the wet gravel of the road. The noise went from rushing water hitting the truck to applause from all the people watching me cross. I knew then I made it and was safe.

After we drove out of the river about 100 feet, we stopped to watch the next truck attempt at what we just did; but they didn't use any helpers in the water. They just saw our success and thought they could make it also. We watched in horror as that truck landed right on top of the big rock, teeter-tottering while the river was trying to push it downstream. Like every truck in Haiti, it was severely overloaded, and everyone in the truck bed was screaming for help, but there was nothing anyone could do. They were already past the point of no return.

As we drove away with my two shivering staff beside me in the truck, they told me that even though they were holding onto each other just inches apart as a pair, each individually prayed to God to forgive them of all their sins—the ones they knew and the ones they didn't know. Both were frightened that the river would take them to an early (and almost inevitable) death. I can't help but think that the power of the Lord in Psalm

41:2 did preserve them, and me too. We rejoiced that night in a dry hotel room as we acknowledged that God kept us alive.

## Whose Report Will You Believe?

Bad reports. I think we would agree that we all get them. Whether it is a medical report, failed relationships, or looking at a dangerous river, they come at us at the most inopportune moment. I don't know which is more painful when a bad report comes; whether we are riding high like on the wings of eagles, or desperately trudging through the mud in the valley of the shadow of death, they usually pack the same punch either way. Wouldn't it be a benefit to remind the Holy Spirit of your commitments to consider the poor and then allow him to work on your behalf? Adverse reports don't always have the last word. God still has the final say. When we are obedient to what the Bible says about our lives, the Word will work as we work the Word. That certainly includes Psalm 41:2 as He promises to preserve our lives.

This chapter would be a logical place to tell of my miraculous healing of COVID-19 through Psalm 41. This book is obviously dedicated to this pandemic that has taken over the world. But it is imperative that you understand the fullness of these three verses that can destroy the works of the devil. I believe a virus that surprisingly just "shows up" is a work of the devil. Therefore, it must be destroyed. Jesus and all the Apostles point to this Psalm. It contains so much power and solutions to a global problem that we all need to understand the extensiveness of it. So, read on as the victory I'm pointing to can be a game-changer, dare I say, life-changer for you and your family.

# CHAPTER FIVE

## They Will Be Blessed On The Earth

The Lord always has a way of teaching me about His blessing over my life. It always seems to point towards His calling for me. Prayer has always been a part of the process since accepting Christ. A simple prayer after years of making pornography and toxic living changed me forever. I guess that is how it's supposed to be when the Lord wants to show His love for us. I learned much about prayer from the joy in seeing the answers. While at other times, it was a lesson taught to me through frustration.

Frustration? Did I just say there was frustration in prayer? Let me explain. Early in my walk with the Lord, our church would come together for prayer early in the morning. Even the times I worked the 2nd shift, I would get up at 5:30 in the morning to make it by 6:00. I would love to tell you that the fire of God fell every time I prayed. Many times, I prayed for myself to stay awake, to be able to pray. It was my schoolroom experience as I watched, listened, and learned how to pray from others. There is no better lesson than to pay attention to those who have walked with the Lord for many years. One particular morning, the prayer was led by one of our elderly pastors. Pastor Stan Crouch was one of the most humble, godly men I have ever met. His many years of serving the Lord shone through his countenance.

On this morning, Pastor Stan said that the Lord spoke to him and said to lay hands on everyone and pray over them. There were probably 30 people there that morning. Stan told us as he made his way around the room for each of us to pray for our church, families, and needs. For me, it was time to watch and learn. I prayed with one eye open, always watching and learning how Pastor Stan was praying for people. I just couldn't wait for him to get to me. After he prayed for a couple of people on my left, he came right over to me and... NOTHING! He missed me completely. How was that possible that he walked right past me? Did I offend him somehow? Was he mad at me? Was I wrong to pray and watch him at the same time? What did I do? Now I was starting to think I was the one who should be offended. After all, it was quite a sacrifice to be able to get there at that early morning hour.

As soon as I reached the level of self-pity where my thoughts were screaming, "How dare he miss me!" I hear a voice say, "watch...". I looked around to see if someone was talking to me, but everyone was praying or going about their day. As I folded my hands again and bowed my head, there was that voice back, "watch...". Watch...? Watch what? What am I supposed to be watching? Then Pastor Stan caught my attention as I could see the sunrise coming in through the window, and it was reflecting the tears running down his face. He was pouring himself out on every single person he put his hands on. Well, everyone but me. By that time, I knew it had to be God speaking to me as I saw this quiet, older man going person to person and praying with all his strength. He wasn't talking loudly, and yet it was speaking volumes to me. I have never seen anyone love people so much. I learned such an important lesson that morning. I truly felt blessed just to be at the right place, at the right time for the Holy Spirit to teach me something I would need many times over in my future.

As time went on, I worked in the television industry and began to feel the call to ministry. But how do I approach that with the church? I had no degree in theology. I had only been a Christian for three years at that time. I didn't know how to preach or give messages, but I just knew there was more. On a Monday morning, I got a call at work from my senior pastor. He said he had called a special prayer meeting for Tuesday evening but explained after the date was set, he realized his prior commitments couldn't be changed. That commitment involved him as well as the associate pastor. He asked if I would step in and lead the meeting. I was so excited I didn't even sleep Monday night. I was thinking about all the different ways to pray. Then came that image in my mind of Pastor Stan. I knew then that all I needed to do was pour out my love and prayers to the Lord.

Thinking of Pastor Stan took the heat off that night. As I walked to the stage to begin our prayer time, both the senior and associate pastor were there. I was quite alarmed as inevitably they would lead the meeting. However, both said their commitments changed that evening, yet they still wanted me to lead the prayer that night. I don't know if this was all a setup, or was it just God's way? I remember taking one big breath at the beginning and never stopped for the next 60 minutes. Call it fear. (more like being petrified) Call it faith. I don't know. What I do know is that I was asked to do more and more. Several months had passed when the invitation came to be on staff at the church.

Because God gave me that moment to observe Pastor Stan, I can tell you that I'm blessed on this earth, just as the promise says. Long before I was "pastor this" or "missionary that," I was just a hungry soul looking to be used by God.

## Being Blessed Equals Answered Prayer

After becoming a pastor, I was at a meeting of elders and staff, and our senior pastor informed us that the present leader of the nursing home ministry had to step down for health reasons. That leader was none other than Pastor Stan. After listening to our pastor describe what was needed, he asked for a volunteer. In my mind, I thought this was not for me. Surely an "older" person should do this ministry and would be more able to connect with, well…older people. To my surprise, nobody raised their hand. As I looked around the room, all I could think about is how I keep saying to God, "send me." So, nervously I raised my hand and said, "I'll do it." I think there was a sigh of relief across the room since there wasn't significant interest in going to nursing homes. Or possibly it was that everyone's plate was full of their current responsibilities. I remember the argument in my head, wondering what in the world I was doing. I had no clue about nursing homes. How could this remotely get me to the place where I felt God's purpose in my life? Visiting old folks didn't fit into this plan. I couldn't believe that I was now the new nursing home pastor. I couldn't perceive it, but my lessons in being blessed on the earth were about to take a big leap.

I was intimidated in a big way as I did my first meeting at the nursing home on a Sunday afternoon. Most of the people who were bedridden or in wheelchairs would just give me a blank stare as I asked them if they wanted to join us for a church service. Some even mumbled some things that I couldn't understand, so I excused myself quickly from the conversation. After walking the three floors inviting the patients and their visitors, I found myself in a room with just four people. Two of them were incoherent and simply stared at the wall behind me. I was happy about that wall, as it separated me from anyone in the hallway listening to the embarrassingly awkward sermon I was trying to give.

After I got home from that first visit to the nursing home, I prepared to inform my pastor on why I had to quit. I also had some mild hearing loss from racing cars in my teen years. I couldn't hear, and they couldn't understand. To me, I just couldn't perceive this to be a good fit.

The next morning, as I went to the church to explain this to our senior pastor, I ran across one of my elders and described it to him. I was hoping he would agree with me and that excusing myself would be the right thing to do. To my surprise, though, he said one sentence to me that made so much sense. He simply said, "To catch the right fish, you have to use the right bait." I can't tell you how that stuck in my head. I couldn't get rid of the thought. Minutes later, the senior pastor asked how the nursing home meeting went. I could sense he was expecting a bad report from me. I paused for a few seconds and said that it went just fine and that I couldn't wait to do so it again. I conveniently forgot to tell him that I had only four people.

The right bait…the right bait…? What could I possibly use as the right bait to get older people to come to the service? Just then, I was startled as my 7-year-old son burst through the doors with his two friends in tow. As the kids said a quick hello and raced downstairs to the playroom, it hit me. KIDS! What better way to talk to older adults than with little children? Before the next service, I called some parents who were more than excited that I would ask them if their children could come to do ministry.

After our church service on Sunday, I brought all the youngsters together to tell them my detailed battle plan. As they all leaned in and waited for me to talk, I broke out in laughter and told them I didn't have a clue. I just needed them to go into each room and say hello and ask if the people wanted to go to church. Now obviously, none of these children had any understanding of medical issues; but if they got a yes, a head nod, or even a grunt, these little guys would take off the brakes on the wheelchairs and started rolling them into the Chapel.

By the time I got back to the room, it was packed out. Instead of just four people, I had four rows of people, all in their wheelchairs perfectly lined up from wall to wall. I looked over at my son in astonishment and asked about all of these people. He had a huge smile and innocently shrugged his shoulders and told me he brought them all in. The outer walls of the room were full of family, friends, and employees who were curious about what all the excitement was about with these boys pushing wheelchairs up and down the halls. Of course, there were a few of the incoherent ones talking gibberish, but they looked very harmless. The presence of the employees around the room reassured me that they were not concerned. Without hesitation, I taught a short message interspersed with stories I remembered about growing up on the river. I seemed to have everyone's attention, but I couldn't find a way just to end the meeting with an "amen." I told the children to begin praying over everyone. It was as if Jesus walked into the room and started loving people through these few kids.

Throughout the time, I was interrupted by curious family members and nurses hustling in the doorway looking for their family member or patient, since they were no longer in their rooms as was usual. Once they saw what was happening in our little Chapel and that everything was fine, you could see their big smiles. Many stayed in the hallway listening to my message and watching their loved ones get prayer. Not only was I speaking to those in the room, but we always had several in the halls listening. Many from the hallway would come to me afterward, sometimes in tears, thanking me for caring enough to bring their loved one to church. I would just roll my eyes to the boys that were with me and tell them that it wasn't me; it was these little evangelists, which amused everyone.

Whenever it was our church's rotation turn to have service, we would fill the room. It was a joy to invite my pastor a few months later to a full house where the overflow of family members had to wait outside the door. We found the right bait to catch the right fish. I didn't have to go any further than my young son and his friends.

What does this have to do with being blessed on the earth? Everything! The people who felt unwanted were loved. An entire younger generation learned to serve. Relief came to the nursing staff too. Not only did they get a break from caring for their patients, but they also received ministry. While in the nursing home, we felt like we were missionaries in a foreign country. Due to some of the medical issues numerous people were facing, we couldn't speak the language but somehow learned to communicate. With many of the equipment obstacles, we found solutions too. More importantly, people young and old found hope in Jesus. Maybe others would have done it differently with some of the more serious medical conditions, but our young team felt we were doing right, and God honored that. Every meeting, it felt like God was pouring out His grace on these lovely old souls. Walking out the doors after the ministry gave us all the feeling of accomplishment. Can you hear the phrase 'being blessed in the earth' in that statement?

## Tying Prayer And Ministry Together

In my first story, I spoke about being blessed on the earth through prayer. My second story was about serving those who didn't seem relevant in this world. Now let me tie them together in a symphony.

In the book of Revelation, the Bible speaks about the prayers of the saints held in bowls. I never really thought of this much as in my mind, it was a future event that I will see someday in heaven. One unique experience changed all of that.

Before I explain, let me paint a picture for you. If you were to come to Haiti and see the area where we work, using the word "blessed" might be a stretch for your imagination. We are in a remote area in the mountains above the coast. Most of the surrounding hills are barren from years of cutting down trees for cooking. We usually have long spells of drought where nothing can be grown. Then the rainy season arrives and brings violent tropical storms. These weather patterns put much stress on keeping our roads drivable. I have been through 11 hurricanes and countless tropical storms. After each significant storm, organizations come with food relief of some kind. Whether the aid comes from The Red Cross, United Nations, or other organizations, this aid arrives in the affected cities. These remote villages where I work would never have access to this assistance.

This is the area where we built a school where there was never a school. The lack of education was evident. Illiteracy and superstition were everywhere. The key for me was when our staff gave out a couple of cases of Bibles. Smiles were everywhere, as everyone was so happy to have their own Bible. The problem was no one could read them. When I would have Bible study, I would talk about scripture, but I always had to pause as just a few educated people had to show others where the scripture was. Picture in your mind a group of 50+ people sitting with Bibles in their hands, and 3 or 4 people had to walk up and down the chairs to show people where to find that scripture. Now imagine a sermon of 5 different scriptures. Let's just say it took quite a long time to make progress in a message.

In this same area, we used numeric magnets to teach the children simple mathematics. In one of the villages, I gave a test to the children. My question was, what is 2 + 7? A little girl came forward thought hard about the answer. Finally, she reached into the bucket of magnetic numbers, and her response was 27. Clearly, we needed a school.

If you walk through a village with me, you will probably question my statements about how "blessed" I am to be there. A typical village in Haiti consists of different buildings made of sticks, mud, cement blocks, and plastic tarps. Undernourished elderly and signs of starvation in the children are common. If the activation of Psalm 41:1-3 is considering the poor, I'm in a pretty good place to start.

Over the last several years, I had been invited to return to a mission conference in Kettering, Ohio. The sermons are concentrated on missions, about which I have much to say. I arrived on Sunday, but I wasn't the main speaker as a fellow missionary was scheduled that day. His message was so inspiring it gave me gas in my tank to continue serving the poor in Haiti. As I listened to his word on prayer, he turned to me, and what he said changed my whole thought process in Haiti.

As I mentioned earlier, he spoke from the book of Revelation on the bowls in heaven. Not one prayer was missed by God as each prayer was contained in these bowls. He then spoke directly about Haiti and explained how the Haitian people in the mountains must have been praying. The elderly generation has had a hard life. They are uneducated farmers that live off what they grow. For years they have prayed that their children and grandchildren would not have to live their lives this way, but without an education, it would be impossible. So, they prayed… and they prayed… and prayed… Every prayer was recorded and stored in these bowls in heaven. When the bowl was full, the Lord looked down and tried to figure out who He could use so these prayers would be answered.

For the Lord to even catch a minute glimpse of me, or that He would choose me, would seem next to impossible. I had been living in Los Angeles, making pornography. Cocaine was sometimes my breakfast, and alcohol my dinner. I was relatively content because there was no moral compass that others would have received from the Bible. Sex, drugs, and rock-n-roll seemed to be the lifestyle I had chosen, and I was OK with that.

Can you imagine the discussion in heaven as Jesus looked at the angels and said, "let's pour this bowl of prayers out on Don." The angels must have been shocked. "Lord, you want to pour *these* prayers on *that* guy?" questioned the angels. "But Lord, he is full of pride, selfishness, arrogance, addictions…uh, and not to mention quite a few demon spirits that live there too." But Jesus just smiled and confirmed, "yes, he is perfect for the job." Can you picture Michael the Archangel trying to change the Lord's mind because he saw several qualified candidates in Bible schools that could answer these prayers? The Lord just smiled and said, "My strength is made perfect in weakness. Don would be an ideal fit to answer these prayers. Pour out the bowl onto him."

September 29, 1990, I went to bed as usual without any sense of what was about to happen. Just like the Apostle Paul was comfortably on his horse on the way to arrest and murder Christians. Acts 9:3 says that as Paul drew near Damascus, suddenly a light from heaven shone around him. That is the same with me. As I was in my bed trying to let sleep take over, suddenly, this light came into my room. The only thing I knew that was even remotely spiritual was The Lord's Prayer I had repeated in a small country church as a boy. So, I prayed that prayer and the light in the room ascended into my chest. Can you imagine the commotion and laughter in heaven as the angels retorted back to Jesus? "Wow, You did it again," and they threw a celebration as another soul was saved that night? From that day on, I have never looked back.

## Haiti Has Become Home

Through a series of events that only God can orchestrate, I ended up in Haiti. Psalm 41 says that if I would just intelligently, prudently, or wisely, with maturity of understanding and judgment, see a need, and then looking at the complex situation surrounding it, think through how I could best, most intelligently, and wisely bring about a successful solution to it, then I would be blessed in this earth.

The "think-outside-the-box" mentality of our vision sees lives transformed every day. Our humanitarian outreach is Haitian-inspired and Haitian-led. Our school is one of the absolute best in education. The ministry to the spiritual needs of these remote villages is working as voodoo loses its appeal. The expansion of our discipleship continues to grow. I have seen my two children do missions work around the world because of what they learned in Haiti. My wife has a vibrant women's ministry and ministers to the unwanted and rejected in downtown Dayton, Ohio. I was the first Christian in my family, and now 30+ have come to Christ.

If we would simply orient our faith into action towards considering the poor, the promise of God says that we will be blessed on this earth. Get ready to count your blessings!

# CHAPTER SIX

## You Will Not Deliver Them
## To The Will Of Their Enemies

I watched a program on how the Coronavirus eventually dies as our immune system overpowers it. The high-end graphics made the invading enemy look evil. I got all angry as these little spikes from the Coronavirus were trying to attach themselves to start doing their dirty work. The natural response of our human bodies is to sound the alarm. This invade-and-defend combat turns into a war that we can't see but can feel as fighting begins to break out between the host response and the virus. Just as the virus attempted to replicate itself and eventually destroy our correctly working cells, here came the calvary. T-cells recognized the invader and signaled white blood cells to form antibodies and began attacking. As I watched the animation, I started screaming, "Die!...Die!...Die!" It was like the winning touchdown of the Superbowl as I jumped up and began yelling in victory. I'm sure the neighbors thought I had lost my mind, but I identified with the death of these tiny microbes that have threatened the entire world. That is a perfect picture of the promise made in Psalm 41:2. This virus is my adversary, and I have yet another weapon to defeat it.

I think we all have stories of spiritual warfare—especially the ones that seemed to go on and on. The enemy doesn't give up easily. If it were as simple as throwing the scripture at him, then we wouldn't need faith. There is a reason the Apostle Paul admonishes us to put on our battle-ready armor.

> "Put on the whole armor of God that you may be able to stand against the schemes of the devil."
>
> Ephesians 6:11

## Hit That Donkey!

One of my greatest lessons on spiritual warfare was taught to me when I was in Haiti's mountains. It was indeed a lesson on fighting the good fight of faith. No, it isn't about voodoo priests, criminals, or witchdoctors. It was a much more stubborn opponent, a donkey.

The Lord has blessed us with people that have fallen in love with the nation of Haiti. We have many teams that visit us from time to time. The Americans that continue to come and pick up where they left off from their last trip are the ones that make an impression on not only me but the Haitians, too. I have had many Haitians tell me that they see the Lord's compassion in the various teams that visit. They understand that their country is in difficult shape. They know that their houses, roads, electricity, water, etc., aren't like those in the United States. They sincerely appreciate everyone who comes. However, when people come back again, despite knowing the difficulties, that is the most significant impact.

Connie is one of those people. She is in the medical profession and has been back to Haiti several times. Her first trip to Haiti was on a medical team. I remembered most of her tenacity to pray for healing over people long before she helped them medically. She has been an excellent example for our Haitian staff and students alike.

On one trip, she was in the back of our big pickup truck returning from a village in the morning. As each person jumped off the back of the truck bed with their gear, she did the same, but when she landed, she hit the ground hard. The terrain in Haiti isn't smooth blacktop or soft grass like we would associate in the United States. The way her foot landed sideways and caused her knee to give out. Since I am not a medical professional, I didn't know how bad it was until an hour later when her knee began to swell. She couldn't put any weight on it at all. To me, this was concerning since any decent medical clinics are hours from our base. But the one thing Connie had going for her was faith. I have never met anyone who had more bad reports come their way and see them overcome than Connie.

As I assessed the situation, I knew that her day was finished. I sent the team ahead to the next village as she requested just two things from me: Some ice to wrap her knee and a tape player so she can play her cassette tapes. As the rest of the team went about their day, I stayed behind with Connie to be sure she was as comfortable as I could make her. As I fiddled around with projects on the base, I could hear her singing praises to God with her music. An hour later, she was clapping and shouting, "Amen! Amen!" to one of her teaching tapes on healing. This went on most of the day. As it started to get close to our Bible study time for the village of Ropissa, I told her not to worry about teaching that evening. I would take care of it so she could rest. Connie wanted no part of that. She would point down at her knee and tell it to line up to the Word of God. She would command every demonic spirit that would try to hold her back to leave. When I see that kind of tenacity, all I can do is say, "Yes, Ma'am."

As we sat in the shade waiting for the team to arrive, we witnessed something that shocked us both. Near our entrance gate, there was a donkey tied up to a tree. That is nothing new since donkeys are used a lot in the mountains to carry the produce down to the market. You would see donkeys much more during the market day than you would vehicles on these mountain roads. Depending on what season it was, they would be loaded down with watermelons, pumpkins, avocados, mangos, and just about anything else that grows well in the mountains. We didn't pay much attention to this donkey until a woman walking down the road was pulling her own donkey behind her.

Now, unless you have seen donkeys fight one another, you would be astonished by the scene this causes. Without warning, the donkey on the road ran over and started a fight with the one tied to the tree. Between all the dust stirred up, you could see each donkey biting each other and trying to kick one another with their back legs. Mixed into this commotion were all the noises the donkeys made as they fought one another. I'm sure in donkey language, they were calling each other every name in the book.

The woman walking her donkey made the best attempt to pull her donkey away, but when they fight, it is almost useless. With all the ruckus came another woman who owned the donkey that was tied to the tree. Now to these people in the mountains, these donkeys are valuable. Without them, they would have no way to sustain a living. She came running out of the house, picked up a rock, and hit the donkey fighting. It didn't seem to faze him as they kept up the combat. So, she picked up a bigger rock, with about the same unfazed results. These donkeys were determined to fight to the end. She then picked up a substantial sized rock and finally inflicted enough pain to the donkey's rear end that it quit fighting and backed away. Within only a few seconds of the combat, the donkeys simply returned to their lazy posture as the dust settled. The one returned to resting under the tree, and the other plodded down the road as usual. Even the women went about their day as if nothing happened at all.

Connie and I sat there with our mouths open. Neither of us witnessed so much violence in such a short amount of time. We were equally amazed at how the entire thing ended with each donkey, and the women owners, returning to life as usual. About the time I was going to ask Connie, "Did you see that?" she beat me to it as we both cracked up. After we regained our composure, she said she had the sermon for that night, and nothing was going to stop her. She told me to be sure not to say anything about what we just witnessed until Bible study.

It was a full house that night under the sheet metal canopy. A cool breeze was blowing through the valley as the sun was casting long shadows on its way down to the Caribbean. The praise and worship that night was led by one of our discipleship team members that brought the presence of God to all of us on the side of that mountain. I introduced Connie as our speaker. I told the group to give her some grace since she twisted her knee and was in some pain. I seemed to be quite premature in that declaration because she jumped up and was a ball of fire that night. Everyone was paying attention as she talked about spiritual warfare and what the Bible says about our victory. Can you hear Psalm 41:2 in that? God will not deliver us to the will of our enemies.

As she neared the end of her sermon, she said the devil is like a stubborn old donkey. When times come, and that donkey the devil won't listen, you pick up a rock and hit that donkey! Everyone broke out in laughter, especially the two women who owned the fighting donkeys. Connie then picked up her Bible and taught that the Bible is the rock. If that ol' devil doesn't stop fighting you, you just need to declare more of

God's Word. That means you've got to get a bigger rock and hit the donkey! Everyone was laughing so hard they could hear us down in the village. She kept on going like a comedian on a stage, saying that if that donkey wants to keep fighting, you need an even bigger rock, and you have to hit that donkey!

When we had all caught our breath, the one woman who owned the donkey that was tied to the tree blushingly exclaimed, "we don't hit our donkeys with rocks," as if she was trying to excuse herself. But Connie was all over it as she snapped back, "Don't you tell me you don't hit your donkeys with rocks. I saw you do it!" The entire meeting was howling in laughter. I thought to myself, what a perfect way to end a sermon and a beautiful evening on that mountainside.

Connie took in her lesson, and her knee was fine that night and for the remainder of the week, which she finished in that very same pickup truck. People in that village remember her so well that they are always asking when she will return to their village.

When Psalm 41 says that God will not deliver us to the will of our enemies, it means just that. When you have a track record of considering the poor, that stubborn devil must go. If fear and torment show up, telling you that you will get some virus and end up like the news reports showing scenes in the emergency rooms across the world, you've got to hit that donkey and declare that Word even louder. "Because I have considered the poor…God will not give me into the will of my enemies," should be our battle cry. Every virus, sickness, fear, curse, and anything else that comes from the enemy is nothing but a stubborn donkey. You must hit it until it feels enough affliction from the Word that the enemy leaves you alone.

# <u>CHAPTER SEVEN</u>

## The Lord Will Sustain Them On The Sickbed, You Will Restore All His Lying Down In His Illness

I can hear the questioning already. "But I have been sick before with an illness. " Even today, you might have recovered from this recent Coronavirus attack, or family members or friends have been sickened. It doesn't just have to be this recent virus. We all could say there were times when we put a title to a specific condition.

I kept these two verses together as they are incredibly powerful when understanding how God comes to you in a time of illness. It is worded in a way that is loving, caring, and compassionate, as a nurse would care for a patient, all the while pointing to the finished work of Christ on the cross. It is the ultimate win-win verse for any virus pandemic.

Notice how David makes the first statement; "The Lord will sustain…" He then makes a declaration as he boldly states, "You will restore…". Both verses are saying relatively the same thing, although written out in two different reflections. If you consider the poor, God will come to you if sickness hits.

There is a printing process technology called lenticular printing. That is a fancy name for picture cards we used to get in Cracker Jack boxes. I remember getting baseball cards that showed the player swinging a bat as I angled the card. The printer takes two sequential images on one piece of thermoplastic cardstock. That creates an illusion of two pictures that move, depending on the viewing angle. There is no better definition of how Psalm 41:3 works. It is the same picture, but it changes depending on how it is viewed.

Let me say it this way. The beginning of the verse is like a huge impenetrable wall protecting a city. Yet, the end of the verse is like the king standing on the wall declaring his protection. Either way, the outcome is the same, victory!

## Fever Shemeever

Several years ago, the Chikungunya Fever made its way from Africa to Haiti. Although it was new to the country, Haitians were familiar with its symptoms since it is similar to Malaria. It is even transmitted the same way through mosquitoes. With fever, muscle cramps, and rash, it mimics what one would go through in the malarial process, with one exception: joint pain that can be particularly debilitating. This viral attack rarely leads to hospitalizations if the symptoms can be treated with over the counter medicines. I think most of our employees contracted this over a couple of years.

Because I'm in Haiti so much, I rarely wear mosquito repellent every single day. I would probably smell like a bucket of chemicals if I did. Many of the different sicknesses and parasites that are common to Haiti have already made their way to and through me. I rarely ever get sick anymore. When the news of Chikungunya Fever was making its way around Haiti, I took as many precautions as possible, but it is almost impossible to stop every mosquito bite.

As we celebrated our graduating class of Kindergarteners preparing for 1st grade, I was not feeling ill in any way. It was an exciting day for the students and parents in these remote areas considering many children never make it to first grade. We were all busy with the celebration, and I was making my rounds of greeting the parents. After a few minutes of resting, I attempted to get back up and continue. The first thing I noticed was incredible stiffness in my knees and elbows. My brain signaled the legs to move, but there was some serious feedback coming from the knees to my brain. I had never dealt with this kind of stiffness before, so I knew that I probably had the virus. Several minutes had passed, and I could feel the fever starting. I began working in the tropics in 2000, so this wasn't as alarming as some of the other things that can be contracted. I just wanted to get to my office and rest, hoping this would pass quickly.

As I excused myself and allowed my staff to continue with the event, I realized I couldn't get my legs to bend up the steps. Just as it seemed that the world started to spin, I suddenly felt an arm come around me and hold me up. It was one of our Haitian employees in charge of the school grounds. He saw my struggle and immediately knew what was going on since so many in his village had this sickness. How comforting to know that I didn't have to cry out for help. He just showed up and assisted me in getting upstairs to my office. He also knew the fever would get worse. A few minutes later, he showed up with cold water and a towel to keep the symptoms in check.

Before the evening came, I was quite sick. I had one more problem, though. One American lady stayed with me in Haiti and was going to help with the next team. That would be great timing making it possible for her to take some responsibilities from me as I rested. However, my rules are very explicit, and I don't allow any women to stay at the base when I am alone. Once we worked out a schedule for at least one of my staff to be staying with her and me, there was no other option for me but to get to bed and be as comfortable as possible.

I felt awkward with no jobs for the American lady in the four days until the next team arrived. Being sick and bedridden for a few days made it very uncomfortable, but for such a time as this, she was there. She made sure every 30 minutes I had water to drink. Then the "nurse-care" definition of Psalm 41:3 started to bring what can only be described as the blessing.

There was a small ice machine that I had used 15+ years before, but it was not working. This helper and one of my staff repaired it, and not only did I have water, but it was also ice water. That in itself was quite sensational.

That wasn't all. Someone from a previous team just so happened to leave an entire box of Gatorade powder mix at my office. Not only did I have cold water every half hour, but it was also flavored and had the electrolytes my body craved.

Still, the blessing didn't stop. Along with the Gatorade was an entire case of single-serve applesauce cups. Now you must picture this. We were up in Haiti's mountains, several hours from any kind of store that would have Gatorade drink mix, applesauce, and an ice machine. What an incredible miracle!

That is exactly how Psalm 41:3 works. Sure, the best idea is not to get sick. The 2nd best idea is, if I get ill, to have Jesus heal me instantly. But neither of those happened. So as the days of fever had to work their way through my body, it was that comfort that got me through. It is still a mystery how that ice machine reappeared at our base. Also, no one from the previous team could tell me who left the Gatorade and applesauce. As well, to have an American friend to help get me back on my feet was such a big blessing.

After the next team arrived, all the events continued without my input, and everyone had a life-changing week. By the time that team was to leave, I was nursed back to health. After this event, I have never had anyone else, whether an American visiting or any of the Haitian staff get sick with Chikungunya. It has now worked its way through the population, and we don't hear of it much anymore.

# Fear Not!

The news is full of a different virus these days. Chikungunya isn't even in the same ballpark as this worldwide pandemic we are facing now. The Coronavirus that causes COVID-19 disease is one of the biggest threats that have happened in my lifetime. It has been an incredible detriment to the health and life expectancy of people around the globe. Not only that, but the financial systems we have all trusted have also wholly collapsed. It seemed at the end of 2019 that the United States economy was as good as it had ever been in some time. Nobody could predict that this one microscopic virus would do so much damage. Many of us were open to considering the poor without much thought. All of that has changed. Entire populations have ceased from continuing in their livelihoods. How the world recovers, nobody knows. Just choose any media outlet, and you will hear of the statistics of this invisible enemy. It is all gloom and doom.

Yet, as believers, we do have great hope. The fear that grips the world doesn't have to be our response. We have an assurance that God is with us. If He is with us, He will provide the power and possibility to overcome fear and live our lives in health.

"For God has not given us a spirit of fear, but of power and of love and of a sound mind."

2 Timothy 1:7

However, if a virus gets through our armor, and by some means, sickness comes to our bodies, our families, or our workplaces, we have this promise that The Lord will come near to us and our infirmities. He will sustain us on the sickbed and restore all our lying down in illness if we stick to our commitments of considering the poor.

Not only is Jesus our healer, but He is also the Lover of our soul. He desires us to experience that intimacy. It's a closeness that is as loving as a nurse fluffing up our pillow as they attend to our sickness. The paraphrase translation from The Message Bible says it like this:

"Whenever we're sick and in bed, God becomes our nurse,
nurses us back to health."

Psalm 41:3

I have to say that if God Himself will be our nurse, all will be well. If any of you have had surgery, you know it is the doctor that does the procedure. But long after the doctor goes home, it is the nursing care we receive afterward that brings comfort as we heal. I'm so thankful that God identifies Himself this way. In the end, we will be raised off the sickbed and have a new and loving understanding of our Father God.

As we head to the next power-filled chapter, let's set our minds to simple arithmetic thinking as we contemplate the promises of God if we consider the poor during this pandemic, or any other time of sickness and distress. I believe after adding up all the benefits, the total gives us the very subtitle this book has been named.

Delivered from trouble

Preserved and kept alive

Blessed in the earth

Not delivered to our enemies

Strengthened

+   Sustained

---

Total:   Break The Outbreak

# CHAPTER EIGHT

## Destruction Of A Virus

I knew it. I just knew something was wrong.

Maybe the whole thing was psychosomatic as I took my COVID-19 test a few days ago without getting my results yet. But why should I worry? Each time I went into Haiti and back again to the USA, I re-tested. The results were negative every single time. My wife thought that maybe I was feeling pressure from this upcoming trip. But I quickly discounted that notion as weeks of preparation had me feeling confident that I had all my supplies. After all, the Christmas events in the mountains of Haiti are our biggest event of the year. Something I look forward to every December.

But something was just not right. Sandee had spent a few days on the couch not feeling 100%, but certainly she didn't look like she was in distress. More just like nagging fatigue. That could be expected as we were both exhausted after preaching four weekends straight. The first church required no masks or social distancing. The next two churches were just coming back from being shut down due to COVID-19, and a fourth was a mission conference where the director called me afterward to tell me he tested positive for COVID-19. Even with that report, I couldn't figure out this dark cloud over me. As I was preparing for the airport, I couldn't pinpoint my exact symptoms or why I even felt bad. I took my temperature several times a day, and everything was normal. I would self-test my breathing, again, no problems detected. I went through the CDC checklist, and all seemed to be well.

So, we loaded up the car with my Haiti supplies and headed to a hotel that was closer to the airport. Since my flight left in the early hours, it was just easier to spend the night and take a shuttle van to the check-in. But as we began to pull out of our driveway, I asked her if she wouldn't mind driving. I felt that I wanted to close my eyes for the 90-minute drive and that surely a little nap would bring me back to myself again.

The opposite was true. When she woke me up in the parking lot of the hotel, my world was spinning. When asked precisely how I felt, again, it was difficult to pinpoint exactly what kind of symptoms that I was experiencing. It was just a bad feeling. But sitting in the car doesn't do any good, so I asked her if she could go check me in as I retrieved a luggage cart to load up my suitcases. Then came my first real clue as my body was shaking in the 25-degree wind. Because of my work in the tropics, I'm usually cold anyway, so this wasn't unusual. But this was different as I couldn't find relief from the shivering. My next clue was when I reached in to get my suitcase as I have done many times before. It took all my strength to lift it to the cart and get to my room and warm-up. Surely after three days since my Coronavirus test, my email would give me my test results that evening, just in case it was a worst-case scenario and I had COVID-19.

As I was fuddling around with my phone, trying to find my email results, Sandee fell face first into the bed. She said she felt exhausted and was thinking of spending the night, as the 90-minute drive home seemed challenging to her. At least some relief came as I saw a new email from the COVID testing facility. But to my surprise, it said, "This email is to notify you that due to the current volume of test processing, your COVID-19 test results are still in process and will be sent to you as soon as they are ready." Here I sat, shivering in front of the room heater, my wife lying in bed, and the weight of such a huge responsibility on my shoulders as we had many pieces in motion for this huge Haiti trip. And I still didn't know exactly what was wrong with me. I knew I had to press into God to get an answer. This required a serious conversation with Sandee as I needed to be alone if possible. She knows how I get in these moments, and it didn't take much coaxing, even in her weakened state, to be in full agreement to going back home. We prayed together and soon we both started feeling a little better. That gave her strength to drive home and warmth for me to stop shivering.

After she left, I knew I had to dig through my luggage to find one of the thermometers I had packed for our school. My hope was it would show normal results as it had for the last few days. Those hopes were quickly dashed as the response came back with a 103.5 reading, along with the screen flashing bright red as if I needed more evidence that I was feverish.

I sat up on the bed with my head swirling about as fast as the questions came to my mind. Should I travel? Is it COVID? Is it the flu? Or is it something that I am quite familiar with, spiritual warfare? After many years in Haiti, I have been conditioned that there is always some type of opposition before every trip. Throughout all these questions that were taking me down a path of confusion, one overriding statement trumped them all and centered me as it always does. I looked up to heaven and declared, "I am committed." If you know of our ministry, commitment means a lot to me. So, once I nailed down my commitment to go, there seemed to be gas-in-my-tank to go to the next level of prayer.

## Read what you wrote...duh!

Suddenly, this amazing thought came to my mind as a lighted billboard had just been turned on. "How about believing what you wrote about Psalm 41"? Duh! I guess that is a pretty good idea. My other books are written about spiritual experiences I have encountered in my years walking with Christ. Then I match those experiences with what scriptures say about them. But the words in this book were given to me by revelation, not experience. When the Holy Spirit began teaching me on this, there wasn't even a conversation that there was a SARS-CoV-2 virus out in the world.

Blessed is he who considers the poor;

the Lord will deliver him in time of trouble.

The Lord will preserve him and keep him alive,

and he will be blessed on the earth;

You will not deliver him to the will of his enemies.

The Lord will strengthen him on his bed of illness;

You will sustain him on his sickbed.

Psalm 41:1-3

This psalm has made such an impact on my life already, let alone at a time of concern that I could have COVID. Typically, in my prayers, I would draw strength from verses 1 & 2. Suddenly, with a high fever upon me, I felt I needed to immerse myself in verse 3. I could feel my faith rising as I confessed these words over my life. Relief was coming in a big way as I could feel the presence of the Lord. I knew all would be well. Then it happened…"bing."

My phone interrupted me by a message coming in. My thoughts went to Sandee driving home, and I wanted to make sure it wasn't her. One glance at my screen and I could see it was from the American couple that was joining me at the airport that next morning. The wife wasn't feeling well, more from the anxiety of the trip than concerns of them having COVID-19. My advice was for her and her husband to pray about it. I didn't mention a peep about how I was feeling.

Then she sent a second message saying she felt fear, as we typically use the sentence "I'm scared to death." I totally understand. The unrest in Haiti and the news about this pandemic are challenging for everyone. But she said they are going to take my advice and go to prayer right then.

After that message, I said again, "I am committed," even though this turn of events caught me by surprise. I settled myself back down in that place of prayer. Again, His presence filled the room, and I opened my mouth to sing songs of worship. Then…"bing."

I thought that sure didn't take long as I looked at my screen again. This time it was a message from an intercessor and friend who I respect very much. He explained his uncle that came to visit them and had died of COVID. But not only that, but the uncle brought it to his whole family. I quickly responded with my condolences and asked how they were all doing. He explained they were coming out of it and wanted prayer for his wife, who was pregnant. Then he closed the message with something that took me off guard. He said, "this has been the scariest thing that has ever happened to him."

Suddenly I was gripped with panic. The symptoms I was having gave me fear. My first message spoke of fear. Now the second message spoke of fear again. The news was screaming fear. The headlines are blasting fear. Can you even imagine all the scenarios that quickly came to my thoughts?

Am I sick? Will I get my students sick? My staff? What happens with the American teams that are coming? What about the 2500 children I am to see in the mountains? And don't get me started on the thoughts of the appalling medical care that is available in Haiti. What if? What if? What if? There have been a few times I heard the devil shout at me, and this was no different. "I've got you now!" Oh, I heard him. The room felt darkened with this sudden apprehension that was all around me.

I want to take the next details slowly so you have a better understanding of how I operate. Trips to the fiery furnace are life-changing, especially when I come out not even smelling like smoke. These experiences have conditioned me to approach obstacles to my faith differently than most. Of course, there are many scriptures on receiving healing and rebuking viruses. But now I have a new opponent on the scene. Fear. And I know him well. Throughout my walk with God, fear has become familiar to me. You don't walk out a calling in the nation of Haiti without understanding this. Do I need to mention raising two teenagers as a single dad? Yes, fear and I are acquaintances throughout my life.

"Wait a minute," I said to myself. "Something just changed." I had a genuine concern for my health, but that was quickly hijacked by these frightening thoughts of terror. The bible says fear brings torment. Abruptly, a battle over a virus took a backseat to the feelings of fear I was experiencing. I felt like a switch was turned on as I spoke out, "no…this isn't right." All this did was redoubling my effort to focus on the very thing I was doing before the phone messages, praying and declaring Psalm 41:1-3 over this situation.

## The Pipeline From Heaven

After I silenced my phone, I lifted my hands to heaven and recited those three simple verses. I could feel the Lord in the room as I reloaded my faith weapon to recite it over and over again if I had to, as the facts that were before me were alarming. I don't have test results saying I'm sick. I don't have any assurances of other believers coming to my rescue. I do know fear came at me in a big way. And I have committed myself to the mission in front of me. With so much to think about, what else is there to do but apply what I believe? These verses contain all the power I need to touch every scenario I was experiencing that night. So, with a little more vigor, I opened my mouth to declare them again.

"Blessed are those who consider the poor…" As soon as I said that, unexpectedly, the room changed. My eyes were glued to the ceiling. It was as if it were transparent, although I still could see the paint pattern of the surface. My eyes adjusted the words coming down from the sky in a circular pattern as if they were spinning inside a pipe. The words were in sentence form of what I just said in Psalm 41:1. 'Blessed are those who consider the poor' spun down upon me and blew over me like a wind from the sky.

"The Lord will deliver him in time of trouble." Again, the words started small as if they were many miles above the building. I could read them as they swirled lower and lower and again, whooshing over me.

"The Lord will preserve him and keep him alive." I spoke out as the sentence repeated itself like the first two, rotating around me as they got closer and closer.

"And he will be blessed in the earth," spinning and spinning around as the words came over me.

"You will not give him in to the will of his enemies," spiraling around me.

I knew that I knew the next verse was a set-up from God to prove my understanding of these verses. They are lifesaving. They are effective in destroying Coronavirus, COVID-19, sickness, fear, pandemic, endemic, or any other symptom or name that the world is screaming right now. Can you hear the news channels as they pump out the dread of a pandemic that we can do nothing about? The only hope they give is masks, social distancing, and a vaccine they blast every minute of the day. I can tell you that God has something to say about that! It is such in the heartbeat of God to take care of the poor that He would back up these three small verses in a Psalm and make them a doorway to supernatural destruction of a virus.

As my eyes are now wide open to my surroundings, I almost couldn't wait to say the next verse. "The Lord will strengthen him on his bed of illness; You will sustain him on his sickbed." That was me! There I was, fever and all, sitting on the bed of illness, watching this display of whirling words coming out of heaven and surrounding me like a mighty rushing wind.

There are theologians out there that could tell me that doesn't happen anymore. Doctors telling me it was the fever making me delirious. Psychologists who would diagnosis me as making up these words. Even the most skeptical person could give me an excuse that this was just headlights reflecting off the ceiling from the highway. Any number of people could challenge me in what I saw. But nobody, I do mean no one, can debate me in the feelings that I have of the Holy Spirit when He shows up in power in my life. Oh, how I wish it were that way every day! It isn't. But time and time again, when all the chips were down, and the devil and my flesh was betting that I would succumb, that liquid light would fill the room. I know what that feels like. Every time that it happens, a miracle of grace takes place. A supernatural encounter that I never can earn or deserve. I felt it before, and I'm feeling it again. Nobody can take that away from me.

As my body was shaking before the Lord's presence, repentance is always the natural expression when His glory is so near. I cried out the 4th verse of that Psalm in saying, "Be merciful unto me Lord, and heal my soul, for I have sinned against you!" Just an hour before, I was trembling from the cold. I felt my body doing the same again, except now before the presence of the Lord. As tears ran down my face, I asked a question that I have many times. Not because I doubt Him. But because He always has the same answer as I ask, "Holy Spirit…do you love me?"

## Where did I go?

I slowly cracked open my eyelids, not being 100% sure where I was at. The room was black except for that bright red led light from the clock radio showing it was 3:04 am. I sat up slowly in bed as the many images I had just hours before were still heavy on my mind. With a quick flip of the light switch, I looked up at the ceiling. It looked like every other ceiling I have seen. Nothing supernatural about that. As the bits and pieces of memories came into my thoughts, I looked around the room, and nothing was out of place. On the table sat the thermometer that was screeching at me a few hours ago. I aimed the barrel at my forehead and pulled the trigger. I anxiously turned it around to see the result—"97.7" surrounded by a more friendly green light. I stood up, interpreting every nerve in my body to point out warning signs that there might be something wrong. Yet, besides the grogginess of that early morning hour, I felt normal. I walked over to the mirror and inspected my face, which, again, for that early of the morning, not bad. I felt 100% as if nothing is wrong. Was it a dream? I went to my phone, and there I read both messages sent to me, but now both giving good news. The American couple would meet me at the airport, and my intercessor friend said all is well as COVID symptoms are less and less each day. There was nothing else for me to do except what I have done so many times before; grab my luggage and head to the airport.

## Cold? What cold?

As I mentioned, cold weather and I are not friends. Temperatures don't have to be 32 degrees for me to feel frozen to the bone. So, you can imagine what it was like being the first customer for the shuttle van in the early morning hours. What makes it worse is that I can't bring a coat with me as my luggage for Haiti always has me stuffed to the limit. As I sat in the seat of the van, ready to head to the airport, the driver said he forgot to sign out and dismissed himself to run back inside. Normally this is a huge setup for pain as my body doesn't react to the cold very well. But as I sat there in the darkness of the early morning, I noticed something amazing; I wasn't shivering. As a matter of fact, I wasn't even cold. I looked up and down my body as this is totally unusual for me. I literally felt like a superhero in the cartoons as there was a forcefield all over my body, from head to toe. To me, this was a clear sign that everything that happened to me wasn't a dream or from a fever. Even after I checked in and made my way through airport security, I approached the officer with confidence as he was taking the temperature of everyone.

## You Are Positive For COVID-19

I hit the streets running when I got to Haiti. I purposely kept myself away from the school since I didn't have the test results to show them that I was negative. I told everyone I was working with, Haitians and Americans alike, that my test results were delayed. But the same puzzled look came from everyone as in one way or another they said I surely didn't look sick.

Three days into repairing the vehicles, I was getting much accomplished. As typical, my phone beeped, alerting me to an email coming in. I was caught off guard when I saw it was from the testing facility in the United States, as I had completely forgotten about the results not coming to me yet. I honestly didn't know what to think as in big, bold letters came the result "POSITIVE FOR COVID-19."

At first, I felt such a dilemma as to what to do. But then all I needed to do was to think about almost every character in the bible who had the same problem with bad reports. Do I believe it or not? I couldn't put out a fleece like Gideon as there was no testing in Haiti. I couldn't walk on water like Peter as this enemy was microscopic. No head to take off from a giant. There was no water to turn to wine. No parting of a Red Sea. No big fish to escape from. I didn't have any of those things in front of me to prove or disprove what God did in that hotel room. What I did have was big red letters saying P.O.S.I.T.I.V.E.

None of us can escape these dilemmas. Whether a bad report on health, family, finances…you name it. It comes to all of us. The great news is that God DOES speak to it, no matter what the details are. He does tell of His opinion. Sometimes as we navigate through life, the answer from God is wrapped in a mystery. But a mystery that is meant to be solved. When it comes to life-or-death decisions, He makes His will easy to understand as He reveals the key He provides to unlocking the gateway to His resolution.

"Blessed are those who consider the poor."

It doesn't come down to His manifestation in the problem. It comes down to ours. How do we show our faith is alive and not dead? The destruction of a Coronavirus has already been accomplished on the cross. His last words were, "It is finished." What Don needs to tackle fear, defeat COVID and receive healing has been done. My responsibility is to agree with His answer and minister back to Him the solution He has given me. That solution is to consider the poor.

# Resistance to Evidence

After a very successful Christmas in the mountains of Haiti, I returned home, and the first thing on my mind was to get the COVID-19 test. This would be the evidence I need to show that God did indeed heal me. But I was in for a surprise. The medical health provider that did all my testing said I couldn't test again for three months after a positive result. Three months?!?

As I sat at home, I heard on the radio of an antibody test that could show that antibodies have been built up in my system to attack this Coronavirus. There were no time constraints on this test as I could get it at my neighborhood drug store the very next day. After drawing a small amount of blood, the technician said I need to wait outside for 15 minutes to get the results. As I stepped outside the clinic door, I stopped to take a glance at the messages on my phone. I was interrupted by the same technician before I could make it 10 feet away from the door. She informed me that there was no need to wait for 15 minutes as my antibodies are so strong that the results came right through within a minute.

This was good news but made me desire, even more, to question if I had COVID-19 or not. The only option was to get a test outside my normal medical provider to come to a conclusion. After flopping down my credit card at another medical lab, the results came within 60 minutes. NEGATIVE

FOR COVID. Coronavirus, defeated. The Word of God, confirmed. The name of Jesus, exalted.

All the questioning in my mind was put at peace as I gazed at the piece of paper that had the answer to my question. Let's face it. This pandemic not only has been a medical crisis like the world has never seen, but also a mental one. When Psalm 41:1 says "Blessed," the word literally means happy. That is a great word when one looks at the news headlines that scream differently.

Before moving on, let me state the heartbeat of God again yet, using a different translation.

Happy are those who are concerned for the poor;

The Lord will help them when they are in trouble.

The Lord will protect them and preserve their lives;

He will make them happy in the land;

He will not abandon them to the power of their enemies.

The Lord will help them when they are sick

and will restore them to health.

Psalm 41:1-3 GNT

# CHAPTER NINE

## Application

This revelation in these three small verses is the undoing and complete disassembling of a pandemic. It is painful for me even to say or just type out that word: pandemic. Who would have thought that this would come at us the way it did? Could it be that God is getting us ready?

> But the day of the Lord will come like a thief in the night, in which the heavens will pass away with a loud noise, and the elements will be destroyed with intense heat. The earth also and the works that are in it will be burned up.
>
> 2 Peter 3:10

Just as precise as I know this virus has done inevitable damage on so many levels, I also know it was no surprise to God. I don't claim to be an expert in eschatology or the study of end times. What I can say is that I pay attention to those whose life focus is this study. As I write this book today, many other signs are happening that are not headline news like a pandemic but just as real.

> (Jesus speaking) "But as the days of Noah were, so also will the coming of the Son of Man be."
>
> Matthew 24:37

God has given us three small but mighty weapons to use in these difficult days. An application can be to any of the end times signs. If a natural disaster were coming to me, I would still be declaring these power-filled promises. Yet, it was explicitly this virus outbreak that the Holy Spirit spoke to me about in Psalm 41:1-3. I can apply these verses with unrivaled confidence no matter what the latest news story says.

Recently our church opened the doors for Sunday services after several weeks of a national quarantine. Oh, how great it was to worship with everyone once more. At the end of the service, a missions-minded friend came forward to talk to me about the news he heard from other missionaries. He asked about Haiti, and I gave him the same tough news as most other countries. I described how the borders are closed, the airport shut down, and foreigners told to find a way out. I explained that even with this grim report, my staff is running everything (probably better than when I'm there), and the ministry continues. Like everyone else, we are just waiting to see what is next. He then gave me a big hug and began praying for me. I will be candid here; he was praying, breathing, and spitting in my face. I'm not going to pretend that the thought wasn't crossing my mind of this encounter. Let's just say there was no social distancing. My first reaction was that we are in church. Surely, I wouldn't get some virus from a brother pouring out his heart in prayer. But there is no assurance in just a good thought. My security came from Psalm 41. "Because I consider the poor, no virus is coming to me, and even if it does,

God will sustain me and then restore me." It brought great peace to me as my brother was as sincere as he could be as he was praying for me.

## Obedience Is Always Better Than Sacrifice

Recently I was honored to baptize several young men from Teen Challenge in a river near Cincinnati. I taught from Romans chapter 6 about the "newness of life" that happens when they come out of the water. All their past sins and failures stay in that murky river, and a new man comes out. It was a glorious time. It wasn't their commitment, understanding, or even agreement that brought that. It was their obedience to God's Word about baptism that this supernatural work came to them. Anytime we are obedient to what the Bible is instructing us to do, we get the benefits. What is a more significant benefit than the promise of three small yet powerful verses in Psalm 41 in this day?

## Practice What I Preach

You may or may not know that I had a marriage of 20 years that ended in Haiti. It seemed always to have its ups and downs. I guess everyone can say that about marriage. In one of the "down" times, however, I found myself suddenly managing the finances. It was an area of our life together that I didn't have to deal with very often since bringing in the funds was my main job. I just assumed what I brought in was paying what was needed to go out. It was apparent that the issues of our marriage would take a little time to work through. As the bills came into the mailbox, I knew I had to start somewhere. I couldn't even remember the last time I opened the checkbook, let alone balance it. On top of that, I began receiving bills that I didn't realize we owed from credit cards that I didn't recognize. Just the same, there was my name on each page, front and center. It didn't take too long to realize that the outgoing bills were coming in faster than my paycheck. On top of the strain that I was dealing with in repairing a marriage, I knew I couldn't just wish this task away. I remember sitting down at the desk and praying. The first thing that came to my mind was to sow seeds into the missionaries I knew of and vouch for their activity in taking care of the poor. It wasn't much I can assure you: $10 to Mexico, $15 to the Philippines, $10 to Inner-City outreaches in Cincinnati. The amounts weren't massive, but after the tithe, these ministries were next. To this day, I recall the release of stress as I prayed over those few envelopes with my offering checks inside. There was an unshackling of anxiety in the marriage restoration process. I can tell you that God showed up in a Psalm 41 way. I didn't pay off all my debts in just three months, although that would not be too hard for God. I found that I was paying all the bills and slowly having a little extra leftover within that time. Even today, I still remember that experience and am never sure how the extra showed up. What I do know is the Lord delivered me in my day of trouble. Something else showed up at that time. Joy.

"Let every man give according to the purposes in his heart,
not grudgingly or out of necessity, for God loves a
cheerful giver."

2 Corinthians 9:7

## Proof Is In The Pudding

As I bring this to a close, the application of Psalm 41:1-3 is incredibly simple and yet extremely powerful. Obedience in verse one brings the promise of the rest of the scriptures. I feel that this was given to me by the Holy Spirit for such a time as this. But I must also urge caution. We must not imagine the power of these three small verses will actively operate to all who casually give to the poor or leave instructions in their wills to provide aid to charity, or some other kind of contributions to societies. As fulfilling as that may feel, this is not what these three verses are alluding to. The supremacy and dominion of Psalm 41:1-3 have the capability to stop a virus from harming you or your family. In the light of what has been shared, we should see no difference in the urgency of Jesus saying to "love thy neighbor" than "consider the poor." Two different scriptures, and yet both point to the importance of understanding. Not narrowing down our focus to this very point will cause us to miss the benefits, both here and in heaven. Jesus brought this same revelation through the New Testament in Matthew 25. The list He gives matches the very definition of the poor in Psalm 41.

(Jesus speaking) "Then the King will say to those at His right hand, 'Come, you blessed of My Father, inherit the kingdom prepared for you since the foundation of the world. For I was hungry, and you gave Me food, I was thirsty, and you gave Me drink, I was a stranger, and you took Me in. I was naked and you clothed Me, I was sick, and you visited Me, I was in prison and you came to Me.'

"Then the righteous will answer Him, 'Lord, when did we see You hungry and feed You, or thirsty and give You drink? When did we see You a stranger and take You in, or naked and clothe You? And when did we see You sick or in prison and come to You?'

"The King will answer, 'Truly I say to you, as you have done it for one of the least of these brothers of Mine, you have done it for Me."

Matthew 25:34-40

Now that scripture is the mirror image of Psalm 41:1-3. In my Bible, those scriptures are 341 pages apart. But they could easily be next to each other in thought and deed. We have this holy calling. One that asks obedience from us, as well, the benefit of that obedience from Him. That is the biblical genetic code in the deconstruction of a virus—the ultimate achievement of breaking the outbreak.

## Consider The Poor = Receiving The Power

If you are like me, even as I write this, I think of those in need. I know I can't fix every single issue in why people are in poverty. But I can do something, even though I can't do everything. The very best I can do is put it in the Lord's hands and believe the poor will benefit from receiving, just as I receive the benefit of giving. I also must use caution that I come off sounding selfish. That somehow all this effort to consider the poor is at the poor's expense so that I can be blessed. That is a ditch we all must avoid. Our hearts must be right in how we apply Psalm 41, as in every other discipline of God's Word. In Matthew 6, not letting the left hand know what the right hand is doing is much more a heart issue than a hand issue. We all need to approach the promises of God just as we are. The Psalmist says only a few lines down from our principle verses:

"As for me, You uphold me in my integrity, and set me
before your face forever."

Psalm 41:12

Let us all commit and recommit to serve the Lord through these three small verses. We need to have peace in allowing the Creator of the Universe to demonstrate that this pandemic didn't catch Him by surprise. Not only that, but I believe that He did provide an antidote to BREAK THE OUTBREAK. By faith, we can operate in His instructions and not be afraid. Like the blowing of the shofar to celebrate God's kingship, let's receive His benefits so that we can do His will. If the media dictates how a silent virus reaches every corner of the globe, we can undoubtedly be equipped to do the same with the Good News of Jesus Christ. Let all of us receive it today.

# About Don Adamson

Don Adamson began ministry almost from the very first day he accepted the forgiveness of Jesus Christ. He needed that forgiveness as, after years of drug and alcohol abuse, he found himself working in the high stakes pornography industry. Years of porn and the fast-paced life of Southern California set him up for a genuinely supernatural move of God, where he turned his back on the former things and now uses his past to help others. That kind of night and day change has led him around the world in ministry before finally settling down in Haiti's remote mountains. Though he declares he will always be a "country boy" from the Ohio River Valley, he divides his time between Haiti and his home in Dayton, Ohio, where he lives with his wife, Sandee. Don has two children who have followed the worldwide missions calling separately and together. His most recent accomplishment was building a school in a remote village of Haiti, where each year, hundreds of children are learning the love of Jesus. These children are also gaining knowledge and skills that will take them out of poverty. They will be the future and hope of tomorrow's Haiti. Acts 29 Missions continues to take the gospel to Haiti's most remote corners where the gospel has never been preached.

## About Acts 29 Missions

The name for the ministry of Acts 29 Missions came in the summer of 2000 as Don Adamson prepared for his first move to

Haiti. After Don left pornography and drugs, God began doing mighty things in his life as he traveled around the world in mission work. It was during this time that God spoke to him about the importance of continuing the work of the early church that is outlined in the Book of Acts. While the final chapter in the Book of Acts is Chapter 28, God showed Don that we are the Acts 29 generation. With that direction from God, Don enthusiastically started Acts 29 Missions with the sole purpose to see the same power Don had experienced in the revivals of the 1990s happening in the church in other nations, especially Haiti.

After four hurricanes struck Haiti in one year, Don and his team were led to the Casale River Valley, where there was no active evangelism work, and people were in desperate need of everything. From the start of doing Kids Clubs in villages to now having a school that is second to none in Haiti, his passion has always been to raise the next generation of believers.

Don has a staff in Haiti that has proven themselves to be nation-changers, but none of the past, present, or future ministry of Acts 29 Missions can happen without those who come alongside the ministry. Getting involved with Acts 29 Missions means that in one way or another, you'll be instrumental in bringing the gospel to those who have never heard it and changing the lives of some of the most impoverished people on earth. Whether you decide to support us financially or join one of our mission trips, you'll be taking significant steps to bring aid and the good news of Jesus to those who desperately need to hear it.

To learn more, visit us at www.acts29missions.org.

To learn more about 4 Points Publishing, visit www.4points.pub

Made in the USA
Monee, IL
06 August 2021